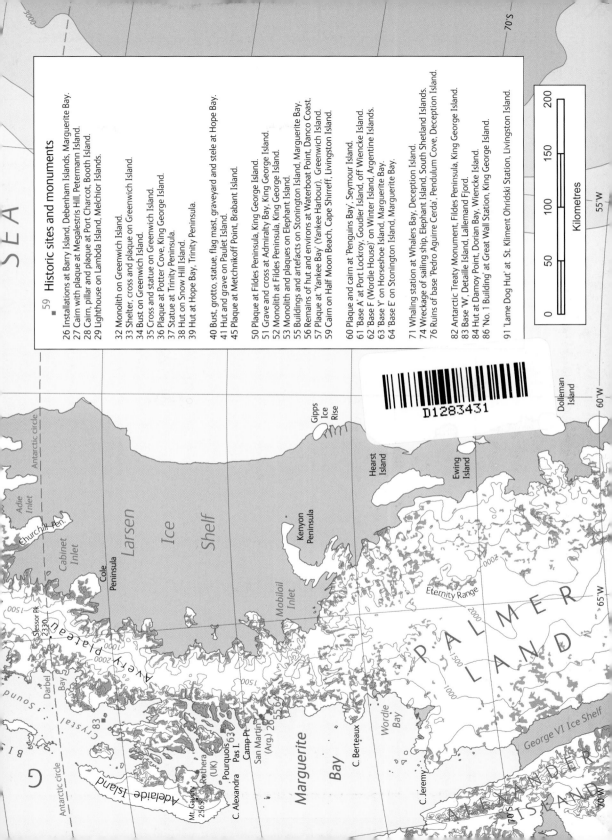

SEA

59 ■ Historic sites and monuments

26 Installations at Barry Island, Debenham Islands, Marguerite Bay.
27 Cairn with plaque at Megalestris Hill, Petermann Island.
28 Cairn, pillar and plaque at Port Charcot, Booth Island.
29 Lighthouse on Lambda Island, Melchior Islands.

32 Monolith on Greenwich Island.
33 Shelter, cross and plaque on Greenwich Island.
34 Bust on Greenwich Island.
35 Cross and statue on Greenwich Island.
36 Plaque at Potter Cove, King George Island.
37 Statue at Trinity Peninsula.
38 Hut on Snow Hill Island.
39 Hut at Hope Bay, Trinity Peninsula.

40 Bust, grotto, statue, flag mast, graveyard and stele at Hope Bay.
41 Hut and grave on Paulet Island.
45 Plaque at Metchnikoff Point, Brabant Island.

50 Plaque at Fildes Peninsula, King George Island.
51 Grave and cross at Admiralty Bay, King George Island.
52 Monolith at Fildes Peninsula, King George Island.
53 Monolith and plaques on Elephant Island.
55 Buildings and artefacts on Stonington Island, Marguerite Bay.
56 Remains of hut and environs at Waterboat Point, Danco Coast.
57 Plaque at 'Yankee Bay' (Yankee Harbour), Greenwich Island.
59 Cairn on Half Moon Beach, Cape Shirreff, Livingston Island.

60 Plaque and cairn at 'Penguins Bay', Seymour Island.
61 'Base A' at Port Lockroy, Goudier Island, off Wiencke Island.
62 'Base F (Wordie House)' on Winter Island, Argentine Islands.
63 'Base Y' on Horseshoe Island, Marguerite Bay.
64 'Base E' on Stonington Island, Marguerite Bay.

71 Whaling station at Whalers Bay, Deception Island.
74 Wreckage of sailing ship, Elephant Island, South Shetland Islands.
76 Ruins of base 'Pedro Aguirre Cerda', Pendulum Cove, Deception Island.

82 Antarctic Treaty Monument, Fildes Peninsula, King George Island.
83 Base 'W', Detaille Island, Lallemand Fjord.
84 Hut at Damoy Point, Dorian Bay, Wiencke Island.
86 'No. 1 Building at Great Wall Station, King George Island.

91 'Lame Dog Hut' at St. Kliment Ohridski Station, Livingston Island.

Kilometres
0   50   100   150   200

55°W

D1283431

ANTARCTIC PENINSULA

A VISITOR'S GUIDE

Edited by Adrian Fox

Published by the Natural History Museum, London

First edition published by the Natural History Museum, Cromwell Road, London
SW7 5BD © The Trustees of the Natural History Museum, London, 2012.
Reprinted 2015, 2016, 2017.

This second edition published 2019.

ISBN 978 0 565 09465 2

10 9 8 7 6 5 4 3 2 1

Designed by Mercer Design, London
Reproduction by Saxon Digital Services, UK
Printed by Toppan Leefung Printing Limited.

Front and back cover: Sheldon Glacier with Mount Barré (2,140 m/7,021 ft)
in the background, seen from Ryder Bay, Adelaide Island.

CONTENTS

INTRODUCTION

THE ANTARCTIC PENINSULA is a 1,800 km (1,120 miles) long mountain chain running north from the Antarctic continent towards South America. It is one of the most spectacular places on Earth, with a unique combination of soaring snow-clad mountains rising straight from the ocean, glaciers calving icebergs into an indigo sea studded with thousands of islands, and enthralling wildlife. There is even an active volcano.

This stark beauty is the backdrop to a fascinating history of human exploration through pioneering voyages and overland travel, bravery and hardship. The spartan wooden huts and other poignant relics scattered along the peninsula, and the evocative place names, are a legacy of this compelling story. Today's modern research stations highlight the importance of the area as a natural laboratory for scientists researching Antarctica's key role in the Earth's natural

systems. Protected by the Antarctic Treaty, the Antarctic Peninsula remains one of the most remote and pristine places on the planet.

Any visit to the remote and desolate, but strikingly beautiful, Antarctic Peninsula is a magical experience, but is enhanced by an understanding of the region's geography and physical phenomena. This guide is written by a team of experts at the British Antarctic Survey and is an invaluable companion to any visit to the region. It is packed with essential facts and accessible explanations and is illustrated with maps and eye-catching and informative photographs.

The first section describes the Antarctic Peninsula's setting in the Southern Ocean, its main geographical features and geological history. The guide then covers the weather and climate, glaciology, icebergs and sea ice. Information on the sparse terrestrial flora and fauna, and a detailed location map for seals, penguins and other birds, show how plants and animals have colonised this harsh environment. A chapter on the impact of climate change describes recent changes in the regional climate and how this affects the glaciers, ice shelves and ecology of the Antarctic Peninsula.

The guide also looks at the human presence in the region, with chapters on environmental protection through the Antarctic Treaty and a summary of the two centuries of exploration and how it is reflected in the place names in use today. Maps inside the covers show the geography of the region and the important locations for visitors.

LEFT
Spectacular scenery of the northern Antarctic Peninsula, looking east towards Una Peaks (left) and False Cape Renard (centre) at the entrance to Lemaire Channel (right).

ADRIAN FOX

THE PENINSULA

THE ANTARCTIC PENINSULA is the long narrow peninsula reaching northwards from the Antarctic continent towards South America. Its northern tip lies about 1,000 km (620 miles) from Cape Horn, about as far south from the equator as Iceland and the southern parts of Greenland and Alaska are north. Slightly closer to South America is the island chain of the South Shetland Islands, about 150 km (90 miles) to the north of the peninsula across the Bransfield Strait. The South Orkney Islands lie about 600 km (375 miles) to the northeast of the Antarctic Peninsula at 60° 35' S, 45° 30' W, at about the same relative latitude as the British Orkney Islands in the northern hemisphere. The isolated sub-Antarctic island of South Georgia and the remote, rarely visited South Sandwich Islands are even further to the north and east in the Scotia Sea.

It is about two days' sailing at 12 knots (22 km/h) from Punta Arenas (Chile), Ushuaia (Argentina) or Stanley (Falkland Islands), to Antarctica, across the notoriously stormy and rough Drake Passage. Icebergs glinting in the distance, the drifting remnants of the last winter's sea ice, sometimes with seals and penguins observing the passage of the ship, and a keener edge to the wind give an early warning of the approaching frozen continent. The South Shetland Islands are often the first landfall, the first glimpse of land being the craggy mountains of Smith Island, rising sheer from the ocean to Mount Foster at 2,100 m (6,900 ft), or the snowy 1,700 m (5,600 ft) summit of Mount Friesland on Livingston Island.

Antarctica is defined politically as land south of 60° South, but a more useful boundary for understanding the characteristics of the Antarctic Peninsula region is the Antarctic Convergence. This is a

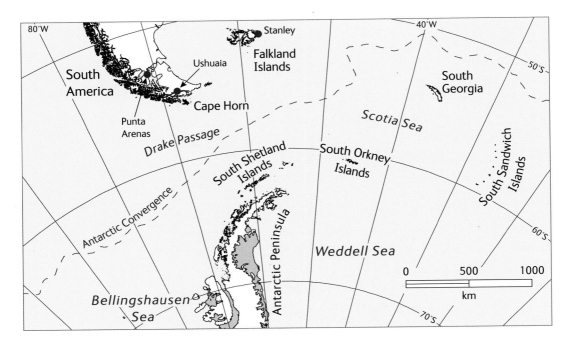

The Antarctic Peninsula is a long finger of land that reaches northward from the Antarctic continent towards South America.

zone, about 30–50 km (20–30 miles) wide, in the Southern Ocean where cold water from Antarctica flowing north meets the relatively warmer waters of more northerly latitudes. This zone is marked by a sudden change of surface temperature of 2–3°C (3–6°F), and acts as a climatic boundary isolating Antarctica from the warmer areas to the north. This isolation explains why Antarctica is much colder than the Arctic at the same latitude. The Convergence encircles Antarctica at varying latitudes; in the Antarctic Peninsula region it divides South Georgia, the South Sandwich Islands and areas further south, from the more temperate areas to the north, including the Falkland Islands.

Physical isolation

This physical isolation protected Antarctica from human discovery until the early nineteenth century, but its existence was predicted long before its first sighting. Ancient Greek geographers had hypothesised that there should be a southern continent to counterbalance Arctic lands, and the name Antarctica derives from the Greek words 'anti' and 'arktos' meaning opposite the bear – the Great Bear constellation in the north. The idea was resurrected during the Renaissance, and following Ferdinand Magellan's discovery of the Strait of Magellan in 1520, Tierra del Fuego on its south side was thought to be the northern tip of this southern continent. This was disproved in 1578 when Francis Drake was blown south and westwards to the south of Tierra del Fuego as far as 56° S, showing it to be an island, with the vast, stormy ocean of the Drake Passage to the south.

Despite attempts to search for the southern continent by Edmond Halley (1699–1700), Bouvet (1738–39), Kerguelen (1771–72) and Crozet (1771–72), this latitude was not reached again until James Cook's circumnavigation of the southern ocean in 1772–75. He fixed the position of South Georgia and discovered the South Sandwich Islands, but despite crossing the Antarctic Circle three times in 1773–74, missed the Antarctic Peninsula because he turned north to resupply. Whilst not proving the existence of the continent, he surmised it must exist as the source of all the icebergs he encountered. He also reasoned that it would be too remote and inhospitable to be useful for trade, noting in his log on 27 January 1775 the now-famous description of any southern continent as 'doomed by Nature to never once feel the warmth of the sun's rays, but to lie for ever buried under everlasting snow and ice'. By the early nineteenth century increasing trade between the Pacific and Atlantic led to growing numbers of ships rounding the notoriously storm-swept Cape Horn. In February 1819, seeking to avoid a storm, William Smith in the ship *Williams* sailed far enough south to make the first sighting of the South Shetland Islands. The subsequent exploration of the region is described in chapter 9.

Geography of the Antarctic Peninsula

The Antarctic Peninsula is strikingly different from the apparently endless and featureless, almost flat ice cap of the continental interior. It is dominated by a long, narrow mountain range comparable in length, continuity and relief above the surrounding terrain with the Andes, Rockies or European Alps. The Antarctic Peninsula as a whole is about 1,800 km (1,120 miles) long and very narrow relative to its

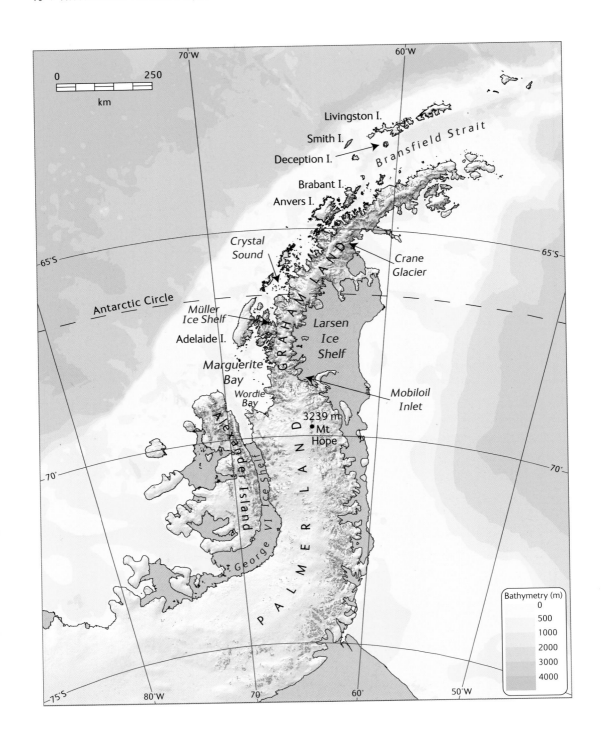

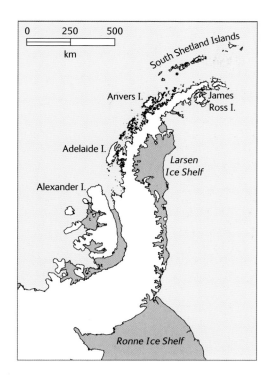

length. The two maps above show the size of the region compared to northwest Europe. The length is about the same as London to Tangier (Morocco), Los Angeles to Vancouver or Miami to New York.

The northern part is typically about 75 km (45 miles) wide, but on a map appears wider than this because the floating Larsen Ice Shelf clings to its eastern coast. South of a line between Wordie Bay on the west coast and Mobiloil Inlet on the east coast it widens to up to 200 km (125 miles) across (see map opposite). This change in geography divides the Antarctic Peninsula into Graham Land to the north and Palmer Land to the south. Despite the significant change in the shape of the peninsula here, it is not a major geological boundary; similar rocks extend south from Graham Land into Palmer Land. This guide focuses on the northern, Graham Land section, because this is the area most accessible to summer visitors.

Graham Land narrows to less than 40 km (25 miles) in places, and until the 1930s the Antarctic Peninsula was believed to be an archipelago of islands. The British Graham Land Expedition (1934–37) finally

ABOVE
The Antarctic Peninsula compared to northwest Europe at the same scale.

OPPOSITE
The major geographical features of the Antarctic Peninsula.

proved it to be a continuous feature connected to the main Antarctic continent. Exploratory overland dog-sled journeys and observations from the expedition's de Havilland Fox-Moth aircraft showed previous reports of channels cutting across the peninsula to be false.

The Antarctic Peninsula coastline is surrounded by a myriad of smaller islands and scattered offshore rocks. The largest island is easily Alexander Island, which is more than 500 km (310 miles) long; about twice the area of Wales, or approaching the size of Tasmania. It is separated from the Antarctic Peninsula by a 25–75 km (16–47 miles) wide sound filled by the George VI Ice Shelf. Other large islands that provide key landmarks for a voyage along the western coast are

BELOW
Straits and narrow channels like Hinks Channel, near Adelaide Island, separate Antarctica's offshore islands.

Brabant, Anvers and Adelaide islands, with their soaring mountain peaks visible from many kilometres away in the clear Antarctic air.

The Antarctic Circle cuts Graham Land at 66° 34' S, just to the north of Adelaide Island on the west coast. It is defined as the latitude where, due to the tilt of the Earth's axis relative to the sun, there is one day of 24-hour daylight or 'polar day' at the summer solstice, which is on 21 December in the southern hemisphere. Conversely, there is one day of 'polar night' at the winter solstice on 21 June. The periods of polar day and polar night get longer with increasing distance towards the south, so that at the South Pole there are approximately six months of polar day and six months of polar night.

In practice, during the high summer between mid-December and mid-January it never gets truly dark on the northern Antarctic Peninsula, even in areas to the north of the polar circle. This is due to atmospheric refraction of the sun's light from below the horizon. The visitor will instead experience a period of magical twilight, rather than true darkness, when sunset blends into sunrise. It lasts for several hours such that the visitor will find it is still possible to read this guide at midnight.

Coastline, ice shelves and sea ice

The coastline is very complex, with a series of peninsulas and promontories separated by deeply indented fjords like those of Norway, Alaska or southern Chile, and thousands of islands, rocks and reefs. A network of straits and narrow channels separates the Antarctic Peninsula and the larger offshore islands. When sea-ice conditions allow, these routes afford a spectacular ship passage. Towering snow-capped cliffs and fractured glaciers plunge straight into the sea on either side of channels that sometimes seem too narrow for the ship to find a route through. Ships today have modern charts and satellite positioning systems, but navigating through the labyrinth of channels must have been a severe challenge for the early explorers.

Close inshore, the first-time visitor to the Antarctic Peninsula is immediately struck by the absence, even at sea level, of any vegetation larger than mosses, lichens and rarely, sparse grass. The over-riding impression is of a stark landscape formed completely of ice and bare

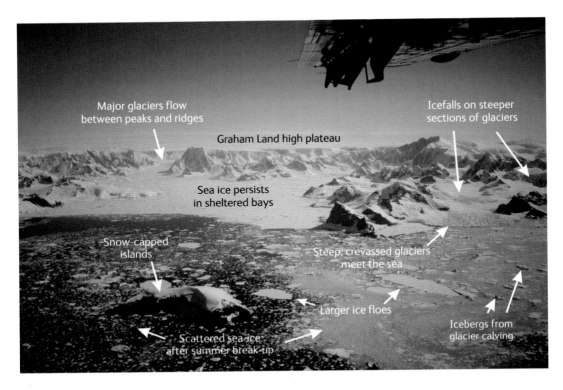

Major glaciers flow
between peaks and ridges

Graham Land high plateau

Icefalls on steeper
sections of glaciers

Sea ice persists
in sheltered bays

Snow-capped
islands

Steep, crevassed glaciers
meet the sea

Larger ice floes

Icebergs from
glacier calving

Scattered sea ice
after summer break-up

ABOVE
Typical mountain and glacier landscape features of Graham Land in the northern Antarctic Peninsula.

rock. This lack of any features such as trees or buildings to give scale, together with the unlimited visibility in the clear air, can make it very difficult to judge distance and size. From the deck of a ship, islands and icebergs that appeared to be in the distance are suddenly near, but other features never seem to get any closer.

There are 10 ice shelves fringing the southwestern and eastern coastlines. The Larsen Ice Shelf, running along the eastern coast, is the largest at 48,000 km² (18,500 square miles), which is larger than Denmark. Ice shelves are formed where glaciers continue to flow out to sea from the coastline, and rather than breaking up into icebergs coalesce to form extensive, flat, floating shelves of ice. The ice shelves can be hundreds of metres thick and extend for tens of kilometres from the coast. There is now only one ice shelf on the western coast of Graham Land. The Müller Ice Shelf occupies a remote bay at the head of Lallemand Fjord, to the east of Adelaide Island at 67° 15' S, 66° 50' W. It now covers an area of about 40 km² (15 square miles) and has lost about half of its surface area since the 1950s. The Wordie and Jones ice shelves in Marguerite Bay had disappeared by 1989 and 2003, respectively.

During the winter the sea around the Antarctic Peninsula freezes over to form sea ice. At its maximum extent in early spring the sea ice can extend as far north as the South Orkney and South Sandwich islands and forms an impenetrable barrier to shipping. During the summer the sea ice progressively melts and breaks up allowing ships to venture along the western and north-eastern coasts. However, in early summer, sea channels can still be choked with remnants of the winter's sea ice, hampering ships' progress. This pack ice can range from large continuous ice floes to smaller fragments herded together by the wind and currents. In deeply indented fjords and sheltered bays the ice can persist throughout the year as fast ice. The bays and fjords off Crystal Sound are notorious for this and Holdfast Point, at the entrance to Lallemand Fjord, is so named because it holds fast the winter's sea ice.

Mountains and glaciers

The spectacular mountains that we see today are the relics of a chain of volcanoes that were active between about 183 and 4 million years ago. They erupted huge volumes of lava and ash that form most of the rocks visible along the Graham Land coast. Today, volcanic activity is restricted to an active volcano at Deception Island in the Bransfield Strait. There are extensive areas over 1,500 m (5,000 ft) high, and many summits over 2,000 m (6,500 ft) reaching 3,239 m (10,627 ft) at Mount Hope in Palmer Land. Mount Français, on Anvers Island, is the highest peak in Graham Land at 2,825 m (9,268 ft). Many of the mountains rise spectacularly from the sea, so that along the west coast between Anvers Island and Adelaide Island there are many impressive summits just a few kilometres inland.

Whilst the landscape is dominated by ice, there are towering cliffs and soaring mountain ridges with exposed rock, so that the Antarctic Peninsula is one of the rockiest areas of Antarctica. About 3% of the Antarctic Peninsula is exposed rock, compared with 0.2% for the continent as a whole. The northern, Graham Land region of the

ANTARCTIC PENINSULA: GEOGRAPHICAL FACTS

Highest mountain	3,239 m (10,627 ft) Mount Hope, Palmer Land: 69° 46' 38" S, 64° 24' 32" W. Highest in Antarctica: Vinson Massif 4,892 m (16,050 ft).
	For comparison: Mount Everest (Himalayas) 8,848 m (29,028 ft); Mount McKinley/Denali (Alaska) 6,194 m (20,320 ft); Kilimanjaro (Africa) 5,895 m (19,340 ft); Mont Blanc (European Alps) 4,807 m (15,770 ft); Mount Fuji (Japan) 3,776 m (12,388 ft); Mount Cook (New Zealand) 3,764 m (12,349 ft).
Highest mountain in Graham Land	2,825 m (9,268 ft) Mount Français, Anvers Island: 64° 37' 42" S, 63° 26' 24" W.
Highest mountain in the South Shetland Is	2,100 m (6,890 ft) Mount Foster, Smith Island: 63° 00' 00" S, 62° 33' 00" W.
Highest mountain in the South Orkney Is	1,266 m (4,153 ft) Mount Nivea, Coronation Island: 60° 34' 59" S, 45° 28' 59" W.
Largest islands	Alexander Island: 49,070 km² (18,946 square miles); Adelaide Island: 4,663 km² (1,800 square miles); Anvers Island: 2,432 km² (939 square miles); James Ross Island: 2,598 km² (1,003 sq miles). For comparison: Tasmania: 68,400 km² (26,400 square miles).
Exposed rock	About 2%, (0.3 % for all Antarctica).
Size of ice shelves	Larsen Ice Shelf: 48,000 km² (18,700 square miles); George VI Ice Shelf 23,880 km² (9,200 square miles). For comparison: Denmark: 43,075 km² (16,600 square miles); Belgium 30,528 km² (11,800 square miles); Maryland, USA: 32,133 km² (12,400 square miles); Wales: 20,779 km² (8,000 square miles); New Hampshire, USA: 24,216 km² (9,300 square miles).

Antarctic Peninsula has a series of fairly flat plateaus, linked by much narrower sections, along its spine at heights of about 1,500–2,000 m (5,000–6,500 ft), with the snowy dome of Slessor Peak (66° 31' 59" S, 64° 57' 58" W) reaching 2,330 m (7,645 ft). Steep glaciers flow down to both the east and west coasts from the high plateaus, between rocky mountain peaks and craggy ridges formed from the hard volcanic rocks. Most of the glaciers are fairly short, reaching the sea in 10–20 km (6–12 miles), but a few longer ones on the east coast, such as the Crane, Flask and Leppard glaciers are 40–50 km (25–30 miles) in length and up to 5 km (3 miles) wide. Due to the steep gradient over the short distance between the 2,000 m (6,500 ft) plateau and the sea, the glaciers are usually heavily crevassed, often with sections of icefall where the glaciers tumble down steeper sections and are broken into a spectacular jumble of crevasses and seracs (ice blocks). Mountain and glacier scenery typical of western Graham Land is shown on p.14.

The average annual temperature is below 0°C (32°F) everywhere on the Antarctic Peninsula, and even at the coast summer average temperatures only reach one or two degrees above melting point. This means that ice can exist right down to sea level, and there are more than 300 glaciers that meet the sea. Responding to the continuous flow of ice down from the interior, the glaciers calve icebergs into the ocean. The icebergs can become grounded in shallow areas or trapped in bays, sometimes for several years, and may be sculpted into fantastic shapes, with pinnacles, prows and arches, by melting and wave action. The density of glacier ice is about 90% that of seawater, so only about one tenth of the volume of a floating iceberg is visible above water, hence the expression 'tip of the iceberg'. Ships and yachts should give icebergs a wide berth because there can be hidden prows of ice under the surface and melting can make icebergs unstable so that they can suddenly roll without warning.

The terrain has always hindered overland travel, and before the era of aircraft, it was a formidable barrier to exploration of the interior and high plateaus. Topographic features with names like The Forbidden Plateau, The Catwalk, The Amphitheatre and Blow-me-down Bluff are evocative of the inhospitable terrain. Most of the Graham Land mountains remain unclimbed, especially in the more inaccessible south and east.

The Antarctic Peninsula offers a unique combination of mountains, glaciers and snow-covered landscape, set against the coastal scenery of an indigo sea, rocky islands, narrow channels and icebergs. All this, seen through the ever-changing light and clear air, makes any visit to the region a magical and unforgettable experience.

PHILIP T LEAT AND JANE FRANCIS

GEOLOGY OF GRAHAM LAND

THE WEST COAST OF GRAHAM LAND is one of the most dramatic and beautiful glaciated coasts in the world. The geological events that created the rocks that form the craggy coastline were also dramatic. At the start of its story, it was part of the great southern supercontinent Gondwana, but became isolated in its present position as other continental fragments drifted away to form the present-day continents of the Southern Hemisphere. Volcanoes have dominated geological events in Graham Land for the last 200 million years and are still active today. Over this time, its climate has changed from a long-lived warm period during the age of dinosaurs when lush forests covered the land, to progressively cooler climates, and finally to the stark, ice-covered world we see today.

This chapter is mainly concerned with the geological features seen by visitors to the west coast of Graham Land; the northern, most accessible part of the Antarctic Peninsula.

Earliest rocks and a supercontinent

The earliest rocks date from a time when Antarctica was part of a huge continental mass known as a supercontinent. This supercontinent, called Gondwana, consisted of South America, Africa, India, Australia and New Zealand, all joined to a core formed by Antarctica (see top image p. 20). Gondwana existed from 550 million years ago until its breakup in the Jurassic about 180 million years ago.

Graham Land has a few exposed rocks along its east coast that date to the Gondwana period. The oldest are Ordovician in age, formed some 486 million years ago, and there are also rocks of Devonian age

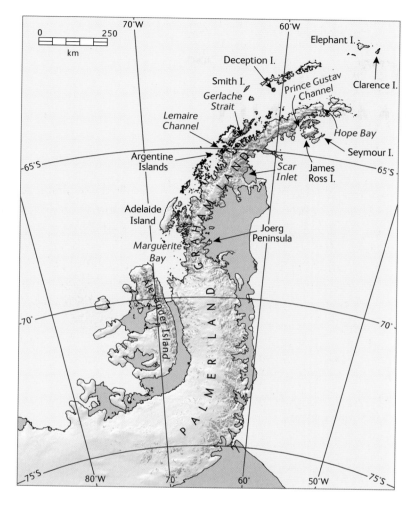

LEFT

Location map for places named in the text.

(about 416 million years ago). These hard, erosion-resistant rocks are granites and gneisses created at depth at the edge of Gondwana and now form rugged nunataks and jagged ridges in the Scar Inlet and Joerg Peninsula areas of eastern Graham Land.

Much more extensive are a group of Carboniferous to Triassic sedimentary rocks called the Trinity Peninsula Group which were laid down in seas around the Pacific edge of the Gondwana supercontinent. These sedimentary rocks were then folded by tectonic events and now form dark coloured, craggy hills and cliffs

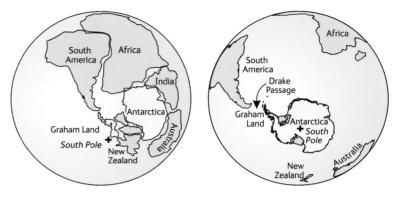

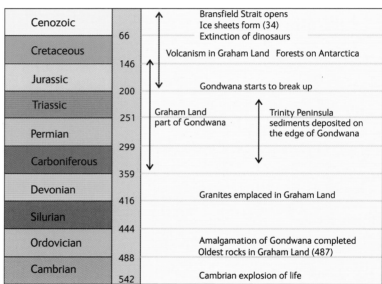

covering much of the north-eastern part of Graham Land. They are clearly visible in the Hope Bay area and along the west side of the Prince Gustav Channel.

Graham Land – part of the ring of fire

Most of the rocks seen along the coast of Graham Land are the products of a belt of volcanoes that ran approximately along the current coastal mountains. These volcanoes were part of the famous 'Ring of Fire', a ring of volcanoes that still surround the Pacific

Ocean today. Huge volumes of lava and volcanic ash erupted from the Graham Land volcanoes, forming volcanic deposits several kilometres thick.

Volcanic activity started about 183 million years ago in the Jurassic Period at the time when Gondwana was breaking up and Antarctica was starting to drift away from the other southern continents. These Jurassic volcanic rocks mainly occupy the eastern side of Graham Land, where they erupted as thick, silica-rich volcanic ash deposits, overlaying a landscape of pre-existing, older rocks. They now form pale-coloured bands up to 30 m thick, with each layer related to a different eruption event.

Volcanism then occurred in the west, and most of the volcanic rocks along the west coast of Graham Land date from the Cretaceous and Cenozoic times, from about 146 million years ago to the present. The volcanic rocks exposed on most of the cliffs and mountains on both sides of the Gerlache Strait, around the Lemaire Channel and

BELOW
Volcanic rocks of the 'Ring of Fire' exposed at the south entrance of the Lemaire Channel.

Rusty patches caused by oxidation of iron in volcanic layers

Bedding picked out by snow-covered ledges

Pale unbedded rock above appears to cut bedding and may be a dyke

Layering

Finely layered volcanic rocks. Pale and dark bands have different compositions

Layered volcanic rocks tilt to the left and away from the viewer because of post-eruption tectonics

Argentine Islands, and south along the coast to Adelaide Island, formed at this time. Some volcanic rocks are hard and resistant to weathering, forming near-vertical cliffs and crags, while others are softer and weather to gentler scree-covered slopes. The volcanic rocks can often be identified from afar because they are dark grey or brown cliffs or bluffs with traces of banding, which are often picked out by ledges of snow. The layering results from accumulation of the volcanic lavas and ash layers around the volcanoes. In places like the Lemaire Channel, there are spectacular cliffs of volcanic rock layers that have been tilted by later tectonic activity.

Some of the molten rock, called magma, that fed the volcanoes cooled underground to form hard, coarsely crystalline granites; these are commonly seen along the coast as light grey, impressively steep crags with no layering. Black, vertical pipes cutting through these were channels, called dykes, which fed molten magma to the surface volcanoes. As the volcanoes eroded over millions of years the granites were exposed at the surface. The eroded material was laid down as sediments in the seas around the Antarctic Peninsula.

All the volcanic rocks, dykes and granites that formed from magma belong to the igneous group of rocks, after the Latin word *ignis* for fire.

On a regional map, Graham Land looks as if it should be a continuation of the Andes of southern South America, and geological investigations have shown that this is indeed the case. Graham Land was joined to Patagonia for most of its geological history, and the two broke apart as the Drake Passage seaway opened about 30 million years ago. The Jurassic volcanic ash deposits that can be found on the east side of Graham Land also occur to the east of the Andes in Patagonia, and the volcanoes of the Andes are comparable to the line of volcanoes that

BELOW
Black vertical pipes, called dykes, that originally fed molten magma to the surface, through volcanic ash layers, as shown here.

formed the west coast of Graham Land. The silica-poor andesite lavas of western Graham Land derive their name from similar rocks that are widespread on volcanoes of the Andes.

ORIGIN OF THE VOLCANISM

The line of volcanoes in Graham Land were of a particular type that erupt above a subduction zone (see p. 24). The Earth's surface is made up of tectonic plates comprising the crust and an attached layer of the upper mantle. Together these are called the lithosphere. Subduction zones are the places where two of the Earth's tectonic plates converge, and where one of them – always the lithosphere of the ocean floor – sinks (geologists use the term subducts) beneath the other.

In the case of Graham Land, oceanic lithosphere of the Phoenix tectonic plate, which from Cretaceous times underlay a large part of the eastern Pacific, was subducted to the east beneath Graham Land. The subducting ocean plate carried chemicals such as carbon (in the calcium carbonate of limestones), sulphur, and a wide range of metals present in ocean crust and its sediment cover, deep into the interior of the Earth. As the subducting ocean crust heated up at depth, parts of it melted, releasing a complex group of trace metals, water and other volatiles that in turn helped to melt the surrounding rock about 100 km (60 miles) below the surface. This molten magma then rose to the surface in pipes and erupted to form a chain of volcanoes called a volcanic arc (see p. 24.). Through this kind of volcanic activity the Earth is able to recycle and replenish many chemical elements in its atmosphere, thus supporting life.

Subduction gradually died out in most of Graham Land, but is still continuing at a slow rate beneath the South Shetland Islands. Around this island group, the remnants of the volcanic arc can be clearly seen. A deep submarine trough to the northwest of the islands is the trench where the Phoenix plate is still subducting.

Another remnant of subduction is a group of rocks that have been highly folded and strongly changed, called metamorphic rocks (after the Greek words for change and form). They form the craggiest islands in the South Shetland Islands, such as Smith Island. These rocks have been called the Scotia Metamorphic Complex and were originally sediments and lavas laid down on the Phoenix plate. When these arrived at the trench where the Phoenix plate was subducting, they were dragged deep into the Earth to depths of 15–24 km (9–15 miles), where they completely re-crystallised to form garnet, amphibole and other minerals that form at high pressure. These minerals make the rocks very hard and resistant to erosion.

In the last stage of their journey, the rocks were exhumed back to the surface as a result of localised uplift. Elephant Island, Clarence Island and Smith Island are formed from these hard rocks, which explains why these islands have high sea cliffs and craggy, mountainous interiors, contrasting with the gentler hills formed by volcanic rocks and sediments on other South Shetland islands.

ACTIVE VOLCANOES: BRANSFIELD STRAIT

Active volcanoes in the region today are restricted to a volcanic rift in the Bransfield Strait. The Strait formed when the South Shetland Islands separated from the west coast of Graham Land at least 4 million years ago and started to drift slowly to the northwest. This happened because the underlying subduction zone created a

BELOW
Cross-section through the Earth showing subduction in action around the South Shetland Islands.

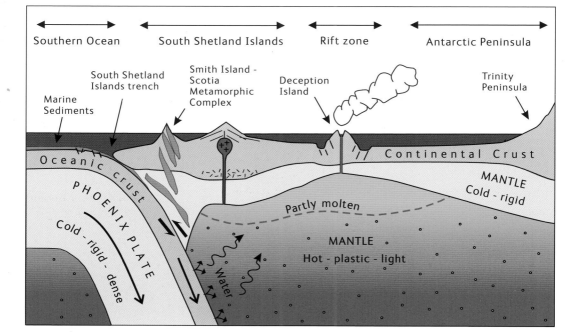

force pulling the overlying lithosphere toward the northwest. This resulted in the lithosphere being stretched until the South Shetland Islands split away from Graham Land. A map (p. 26) of the seafloor topography of the Bransfield Strait shows clearly the active volcanic rift, picked out by NW-SE-trending faults.

Three currently dormant submarine volcanoes, The Axe, Three Sisters and Orca, lie along this volcanic line and rise some 600 m above the surrounding seafloor. Orca and The Axe both have summit craters 2 km (1–1½ miles) across. Deception Island is the southernmost and largest of the line of volcanoes that lie along the rift.

ABOVE

Mountainous Smith Island which consists of rocks generated at high pressure that are resistant to erosion.

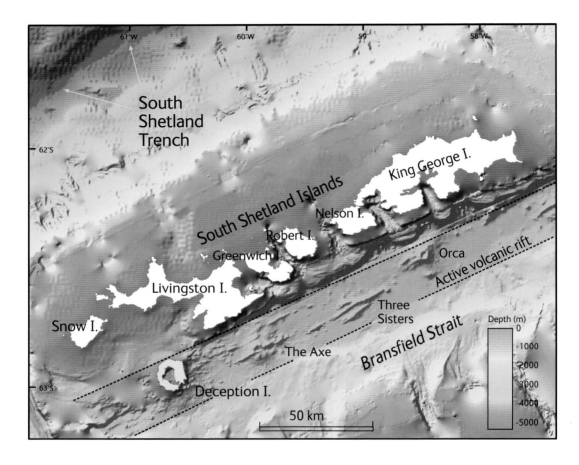

Fossils and the changing climate

While volcanoes were active in Graham Land, layers of ash and sediments from erosion of the volcanoes were deposited in the surrounding shallow seas. These sediment and ash layers preserve a rich fossil record. The sediments range in age from about 183 million years ago (Jurassic period) to Cenozoic times and are preserved in three main areas: the South Shetland Islands, James Ross Island and, further south, eastern Alexander Island. Fossils are important in determining the age of sediments that contain them and provide valuable information on the evolution of life, the origin of present day species in the Antarctic and how past environments and climates were different from today.

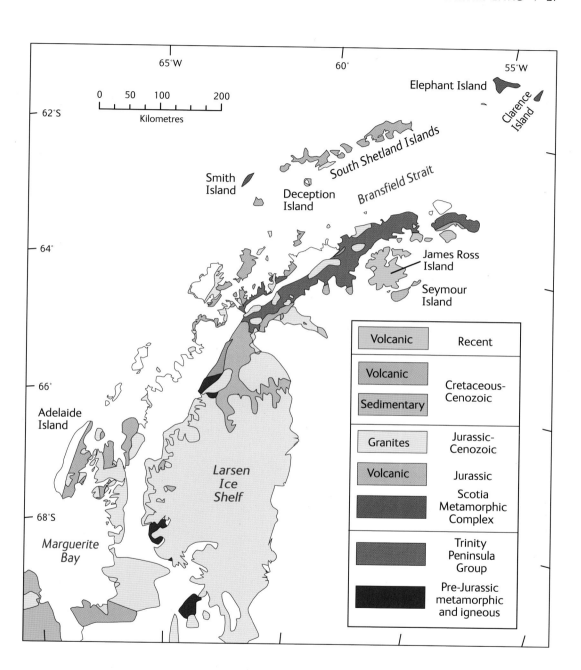

A geological sketch map of
Graham Land.

DECEPTION ISLAND

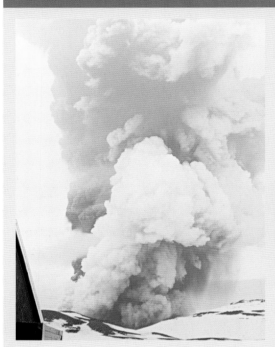

The most recently active volcano in the Antarctic Peninsula region is Deception Island, to the south of the South Shetland Islands. The island contains an 8 km (5 miles) wide volcanic crater flooded by the sea that now forms a central lagoon, called Port Foster. It is reached through a narrow channel named Neptunes Bellows by whalers after the gusts of wind that can blast through it. The crater is an example of a collapsed caldera, formed by sinking of the central part of the volcano, in this case after eruption of a 30 km³ (7 cubic miles) ash

ABOVE AND RIGHT Deception Island during the 1967 to 1968 eruption, close to the UK station. Powerful explosions produced a large ash-laden cloud that rose vertically, while blasts spread out along the ground.

The study of fossil plants and animals from Antarctica that are similar to ones alive today allows us to build a picture of the climate and environment in the past.

The Late Jurassic to Early Cretaceous (160–100 million years ago) sediments of the Fossil Bluff Group on Alexander Island contain some of the most abundant and diverse fossil material on the Antarctic Peninsula. The sedimentary rocks comprise fine- to coarse-grained sandy and muddy sediments deposited near the volcanic area of Palmer Land. There are many fossils of marine bivalves, ammonites, urchins and starfish, which once lived in shallow, warm seas in this region. There are also layers of rocks that contain large

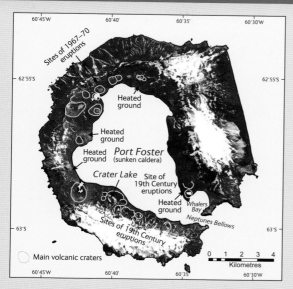

Sites of 1967–70 eruptions

Heated ground

Heated ground

Heated ground

Port Foster (sunken caldera)

Crater Lake Site of 19th Century eruptions

Heated ground Whalers Bay

Neptunes Bellows

Sites of 19th Century eruptions

Main volcanic craters

0 1 2 3 4
Kilometres

ABOVE A satellite image of Deception Island showing key volcanic features.

The Deception Island volcano erupted several times in 1967 and again in 1968 and 1970, producing powerful explosions, dense clouds of black basalt cinders and ash, and mudflows that consisted of mixtures of ash and melted glacier ice (see images opposite). Two research stations, belonging to the UK and Chile, were damaged and abandoned following the eruptions.

Hot springs in the central lagoon today, fed by water heated within the volcano, show that Deception Island is still underlain by hot molten rock. A report from 1921, by the Falkland Islands magistrate and government naturalist in the South Shetland Islands, records that the hulls of whaling ships anchored in the natural harbour of Port Foster had their paint blistered by the hot springs. Movements of the molten magma causes the sea floor to rise and fall in the lagoon, and there are alarming reports of whaling ships anchored in the bay being left floating, with their anchors dangling, by sudden drops in the sea floor.

The historical record is too short to be certain of a pattern, but geologists think that the volcano usually erupts a couple of times per century, and so another eruption is likely in the near future.

deposit. Many smaller eruptions have since produced a large number of smaller calderas and volcanic cones consisting mostly of fine-grained, finely-layered volcanic ash, locally altered to rusty colours and a yellow, clayey material called palagonite.

fossil tree trunks, which are the remains of forests that once covered the Peninsula in warmer climates.

In the South Shetland Islands the main fossil locality is at Byers Peninsula on Livingston Island, where Early Cretaceous sediments contain a mainly bivalve fauna. Sediments that were laid down east of the volcanic arc are exposed in the James Ross Basin. They span the boundary between the Cretaceous and Cenozoic periods, which is marked by a global extinction event that included the disappearance of the dinosaurs. A remarkable series of sediments recording the time of extinction, at about 66 million years ago, are found on Seymour Island, east of James Ross Island.

a

b

c

d

e

f

These sediments contain fossil plants as well as the shelly fauna. Plant fossils include petrified wood, pollen, spores and leaf impressions. A rich variety of fossil plants including conifers, cycads, and ginkgo trees, as well as ferns and mosses, are preserved in Cretaceous rocks from Alexander Island and the South Shetland Islands. Angiosperms (flowering plants), including the southern beech *Nothofagus*, appeared during the Cretaceous period. Extensive forests, similar to those found in New Zealand and southern South America today, were able to grow in Graham Land, because the climate was much warmer than that of today, despite it being at a similar latitude. Global temperatures were warmer too.

The climate of Antarctica cooled in Cenozoic times, and by 34 million years ago large ice sheets had appeared in Antarctica. The movement of ice carved out a new glaciated landscape in Graham Land with spectacular fjords, and jagged mountain peaks formed by hard, resistant rock types – a truly spectacular marriage of geology and glaciology.

OPPOSITE

Antarctic fossils: (a) *Sterculia* leaf from James Ross Island, 4.5 cm (2 in) long; (b) Cretaceous petrified tree trunk, 0.5 m (1 ft 7 in) tall, from Seymour Island; (c) Cretaceous gastropod (marine snail) with original shell material, 8 cm (3 in) tall, from Seymour Island; (d) Cretaceous whelk, 10 cm (4 in) long, from Seymour Island; (e) Cretaceous ammonite, 6 cm (2½ in) in diameter, from Seymour Island; (f) Cretaceous crab claw, 5 cm (2 in) long, from Seymour Island.

JON SHANKLIN

WEATHER AND CLIMATE

Antarctic weather

The visitor to the Antarctic Peninsula will encounter a wide range of weather, often during the same day! Clear blue skies and calm seas can change to overcast with high wind within the space of a few hours. The first sign of such a change in the sky may be seen when tendrils of cirrus cloud begin to invade, followed by the milky white of high cirrostratus. Often this gives an intense halo round the sun, and occasionally more unusual optical phenomena. Then the cloud thickens further and drops lower, the mountains become obscured, the wind increases in strength and finally the rain or snow comes driving in.

This weather sequence is typical of low-pressure systems or depressions, which are the dominant influence on the weather of the Antarctic Peninsula. They extend over a thousand kilometres (625 miles) or more in the zone between about 50°S and the Antarctic margin, often with several encircling the continent at any one time. The atmospheric pressure in this circumpolar belt is generally lower than in the equivalent Northern Hemisphere region, and so central pressures below 940 hPa (equivalent to millibars) are not uncommon and Rothera Research Station has recorded a very low reading of 922.1 hPa, compared with a typical value of 975 hPa for a depression over northern Europe.

The Antarctic Peninsula is the only land between latitudes 60°S and 70°S and acts as a barrier to the progress of the low pressure systems from west to east; the depressions are either deflected along it or reform on the other side. The main part of the Antarctic continent also acts as a barrier itself, because it rapidly rises from the coast to the

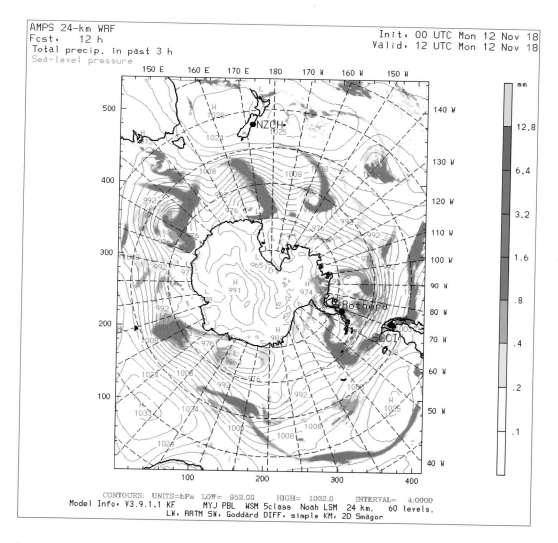

high plateau, and depressions, and the precipitation they bring, rarely penetrate far inland. This is one reason why the bulk of the continent is a virtual desert, despite the great thickness of ice.

PRECIPITATION: RAIN AND SNOW

In the interior of the continent, precipitation (snow) is the equivalent of only around 50 mm (2 in) of rain a year, about as much as the central Sahara desert. By contrast, precipitation at the coast is much

ABOVE

Forecast chart showing depressions (green areas) circling Antarctica on 12 November 2018.

higher, and snow accumulation on the Antarctic Peninsula mountains can be over ten metres a year, equivalent to about 2000–3000 mm (78–117 in) of rain.

Low stratus cloud, below 300 m (1000 ft) is a common feature of the Antarctic Peninsula and has long been known as 'Mank' to Antarctic travellers. It rarely produces much precipitation, but often hides higher rain or snow-bearing cloud above. At Vernadsky station on the Argentine Islands, mid-way along the Antarctic Peninsula, snow or sleet falls on around 250 days a year, whilst rain falls on around 90. Some days get both types of precipitation! Most snow on the Antarctic Peninsula occurs during storm events, and these lead to high accumulation on the west facing mountain slopes. The nature of the snow is quite variable. It is said that the Inuit have 100 words for snow (an urban myth) and there are certainly many different adjectives that can describe Antarctic snow.

Snow is formed in clouds when the air temperature is below zero and there is enough moisture in the atmosphere for tiny super-cooled water droplets to freeze onto particles, called nuclei, of dust, sea-salt, or even marine diatoms, in the atmosphere. Depending on the conditions, the ice crystals may remain small, grow into prisms or needles, or merge together to form larger snowflakes. The shape of the ice crystals is controlled by the form of H_2O (water) molecules, where the two hydrogen atoms are approximately 105 degrees apart. This is close to the 120 degree internal angle in a hexagon and so ice crystals adopt a hexagonal structure. Simple hexagonal crystals tend to form when the humidity is low, but these grow dendritic arms on their faces when humidity is higher. With random chance playing a part, no two such flakes are ever identical and they can adopt a myriad of beautiful, delicate forms.

If the temperature is sufficiently low, ice crystals can grow directly from the water vapour in the air, even under otherwise clear sky conditions. These small crystals float down from the sky, giving the phenomena of diamond dust, with each crystal reflecting and refracting the sunlight like a tiny diamond. At the other extreme, under calm conditions when the humidity is high and the temperature not far from freezing, snowflakes can grow almost to the size of a CD.

LEFT
Photo-micrographs showing the formation of snow. Ice crystals start to form around dust or sea salt particles as simple hexagonal shapes (a). If conditions persist other crystals start to accrete onto the first crystal (b) and more complex snow crystals begin to emerge (c, bottom left). Finally, as accretion continues the snowflakes form complex, beautiful shapes, always based on a hexagon (d, e, f).

Some atmospheric conditions can generate other forms of solid precipitation than snow:

- Rime: where water vapour condenses to tiny droplets that freeze onto a cold surface, such as ship's metalwork, and accumulate.
- Graupel: where the surface is a pre-existing snow-flake or ice crystal; graupel particles are fairly light, like polystyrene beads.
- Hail: grown by accretion of super-cooled water; hail stones are quite dense.
- Ice-pellets: snow or graupel that has been melted, then refrozen.

When it is cold enough on the ground the snow may remain as a dry powder that squeaks when you walk on it, though as it ages the particles get cemented together – the beginning of the transformation into glacier ice (see p. 53). Large snowflakes are more likely when the temperature is not far below zero, and as these accumulate the snow is often good for making snowballs. Fallen snow mainly disappears through the familiar process of melting to slush and then water, however on sunny but cold days the snow can evaporate directly from a solid to water vapour through a process called sublimation.

OPTICAL PHENOMENA

Reflections and refractions from ice crystals in the atmosphere can create intense optical displays around the sun. Most commonly seen is the halo forming a ring around the sun with a radius of 22° related to the hexagonal shape of the crystals. This shows faint colours with blue on the outside and red on the inside, the opposite to a rainbow. Inside the halo the sky is darker than the sky on the outside, because light from this area has been scattered to form the halo (below).

On the circle either side of the sun you may see a parhelion (or sun dog), and perhaps a parhelic circle running around the horizon. Above the sun may be the rainbow-like band of the circumzenithal arc, which often fools people into thinking that they have seen a rainbow, despite the colour sequence being in reverse order. Rainbows themselves are fairly common, and if you pass through coastal channels such as the Lemaire Channel on a day with low lying banks of thin fog with the sun breaking through, you may see a colourless fog-bow.

Other optical effects abound, related to the clarity and dryness of the air and the presence of layers at different temperatures. On many occasions, the Antarctic Peninsula mountains appear from a distance to be higher than they really are, with towering cliffs presenting a challenge for mountaineers. In reality the atmosphere has acted as a lens,

RIGHT
A complex halo display seen at Rothera, showing parhelia, the 22° halo, the 46° halo and the upper arcs of the 22° halo and the circumzenithal arc.

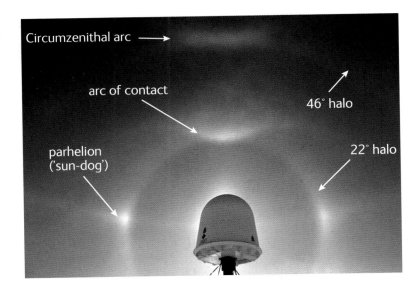

Circumzenithal arc ⟶

arc of contact

46° halo

parhelion ('sun-dog')

22° halo

magnifying a small feature into something much larger. Sometimes the magnification is variable, or even creates a mirror image, and this can conjure what appears to be a 'fairy castle' in the air – the mirage known as fata morgana. The atmosphere can also act like a prism, so that as the Sun sets (or rises) over a distant horizon, its light is spread into a spectrum. As the final bit of the sun sets, red is below the horizon and the blue light is scattered by the atmosphere, giving an intense green flash. At the south pole, this effect has been known to persist for over 24 hours!

SHADOW EFFECTS

Looking away from the setting sun, at dusk the Antarctic visitor may see a greyish band near the horizon, which elsewhere you might think was polluted air. In the pristine Antarctic, where visibility can be over 100 km (60 miles), this cannot be the case, and the grey band is in fact the Earth's shadow slowly rising up in the twilight. Another shadow effect sometimes seen on a day with broken clouds is crepuscular rays – these are bright sunlit areas streaming between darker cloud-shadowed areas.

Under cloudy skies at sea the visitor may see ice-blink or water-sky. The brightness of clouds depends in part on what is underneath them. If there is sea ice underneath, around 90% of the light is reflected back towards the clouds, making them appear bright. If on the other hand there is open sea underneath, less than 30% of the light is reflected and the clouds appear dark. Navigators still make use of these effects; a distant brightening of the sky indicates ice ahead, and once stuck in ice, looking at the sky above can provide a map of where there is open water and a way out.

FOG

When weather systems bring in cold, dry air over the open leads or ocean, sea-smoke will form. Moisture evaporates from the water surface, and then condenses to form fog droplets that look like smoke drifting over the surface. In dense fog, or when uniform cloud covers the sky, and the wind whips up fallen snow into blowing snow above head height, all contrast between surface features disappears in the resulting whiteout. In these conditions the traveller on foot quickly loses all sense of direction and risks stumbling over now invisible lumps or hollows in the snow surface.

ABOVE
Ice-blink heading north
through The Gullet, a narrow
channel between Adelaide
Island and Arrowsmith
Peninsula. The lighter sky
on the horizon shows the
presence of sea ice ahead.

CLOUDSCAPES

Cloudy skies are the norm for the Antarctic Peninsula, with the cloudiest conditions in the north, which is most subject to the maritime influence, and least cloudy in the south, where there is more continental influence.

Meteorologists usually divide up the clouds into three sections of the atmosphere: low clouds which may go up to 6000 ft, medium-level clouds up to 12,000' and high cloud up to 30,000'. The low clouds include the stratus (stratus means layer in Latin), and also cumulus and stratocumulus clouds. The stratocumulus is probably the second most common form in the Antarctic after low-level stratus cloud, and with a low sun and calm seas can give a beautiful pastel effect to the scenery. Cumulus clouds are less frequent as there is usually less energy available to start the convection that creates them. On rare occasions, the atmospheric conditions may combine with the mountainous terrain of the Peninsula to producing towering columns of cumulus cloud.

The main rain and snow bearing clouds form in the middle level: nimbostratus and altostratus. Both are quite featureless and because they are often thick can produce considerable precipitation. Also at this level are the altocumulus clouds. The convection at this height may be caused by instability in the atmosphere, or it may be forced by the mountains of the Peninsula.

Depression systems usually bring with them strong winds, which are forced to rise by the Antarctic Peninsula mountain chain. When air rises it cools, and this increases the relative humidity of the air. If the humidity passes the saturation point, clouds will form. Such regions of saturated air often happen in separate layers, and this combined with downdrafts over the mountains gives rise to wave clouds. Technically these are called *Altocumulus lenticularis*, and often take the form of lens-shaped 'almonds' or 'fishes'. Occasionally, in ideal conditions, spectacular displays resembling stacks of plates or fantastic spaceships can occur. Because all the water droplets are a similar size, they often show pastel shades of iridescence round their margins.

BELOW
Lenticular clouds near Rothera Research Station, with cirrus and cirrostratus cloud above.

Higher still are cirrus, cirrostratus and more rarely cirrocumulus. The cirrus often forms in hooks and wisps, whilst the cirrostratus forms larger patches or a featureless layer of milky white. Both these cloud forms can give optical phenomena, though they are usually more complete with the cirrostratus. Cirrocumulus clouds are rare and short-lived, but can form when patches of cirrus are breaking up.

The summer visitor may spot noctilucent clouds, which form high in the atmosphere at around 80 km, far higher than the highest cirrus clouds. These clouds begin to form about a month before the summer solstice, and their season ends roughly six weeks after the solstice. At the altitude of the clouds, the temperature is at its lowest during this period (below -120°C), some six months after the lowest temperature is reached at the ground. The clouds are usually very thin, and can only be seen an hour or so after sunset (or before sunrise), usually low on the southern horizon. They are so high that they are still sunlit, even though the brightest stars are visible from the ground. They show a silvery-blue colour due to absorption of sunlight by ozone and often form intricate patterns due to density waves moving through the air at high altitude. Occasionally, during an intense display, they are seen over a much wider part of the sky. Their frequency seems to have increased, and they are an indicator of change in the atmosphere.

WIND AND STORMS

The Antarctic Peninsula is a windy place, and still days are rare. Even on bright sunny days there is often a steady 10 knot (18 km/h) wind. The frequent storms often bring winds that can reach 50–60 knots (up to 100 km/h) for sustained periods, with gusts of 70–80 knots (110–130 km/h) possible. Katabatic winds, where cold air flows downhill, warming as it does so and creating turbulence may generate equally strong gusts. These gusts can come with little warning, reach speeds of over 100 km/h, and cause problems for any yachts close inshore or tented field camps in their path. These same strong winds gusting down mountain passes and onto the sea surface, can whip up spray in a gust front or williwaw.

The prevailing wind direction at any location is a combination of the mean pressure field and the local topography, complicated by the interaction with low pressure systems. The Antarctic Peninsula itself creates a barrier to the mean westerly flow, forcing air northwards and distorting the mean pressure field compared to further north. Typically, the mean wind speed at Peninsula locations is around 10 knots consistently from the north-west or south-east, but topography can force this to north-east and south-west. The number of gales, defined as wind speeds above 34 knots (62 km/h) can vary enormously. Vernadsky station is comparatively sheltered and has an average of 10 gales per year, whilst Rothera Research Station receives around 70.

Although storms are a common feature at any time of year along the Antarctic Peninsula, thunderstorms are very rare. In summer there is not enough solar energy coming through the atmosphere to drive convection strongly enough to create the cumulo-nimbus clouds that form the storm cells. Occasionally the air itself is sufficiently unstable for a little convection to create towering pillars of cumulus, which make a strange spectacle along the coast. What can cause a thunderstorm is the instability between cold and warm air masses along a frontal system and this can create rapid enough mixing to give separation of electric charges followed by discharge in a flash of lightning.

WEATHER STATIONS

Most of the research stations along the Antarctic Peninsula make meteorological measurements, which are transmitted to forecasting centres, mostly in the northern hemisphere, over the meteorological equivalent of the internet, known as the Global Telecommunications System or GTS. The manned stations are augmented by a network of automatic stations widely spaced along the Peninsula. All make the same basic measurements – pressure, temperature, humidity, wind speed and direction, and a human observer may add cloud details, weather and visibility.

The amount of precipitation is difficult to measure, because light snow in strong winds is difficult to catch in a traditional rain-gauge. Some progress towards more reliable measurement is being made by using laser systems to measure the size and density of precipitation falling through a beam.

Climate

The climate of an area is the sum of its weather averaged over many years; the standard period for meteorologists is 30 years.

Together, meteorological readings from manned stations and ships, records from automated weather stations, and average surface temperatures calculated from temperature profiles in boreholes drilled into ice sheets, give enough information to map the climate patterns on the Antarctic Peninsula and act as a baseline for measuring changes.

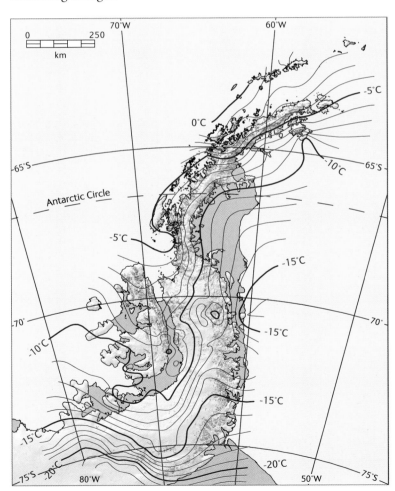

RIGHT
Isotherm map of average annual temperature.

OPPOSITE
Meteorologist Daniel Rylett reads instruments measuring temperature and relative humidity at Rothera Research Station. Wind and sunshine sensors are on the top of the tower, with a present weather detector and laser cloud-base recorder to the left of the tower.

Some key points are as follows:

- The isotherm (contour) map in p. 42 shows that average annual temperature is below freezing point everywhere on the Antarctic Peninsula, including the South Shetland Islands.
- It is colder in the south and east. The average annual temperature at Marambio on the east coast is 4°C (7.2°F) lower than at Rothera on the west coast, even though it is 350 km (217 miles) further north.
- The average monthly temperature ranges are only a few degrees, but there is much more variation in the maximum and minimum temperatures experienced within each month (opposite).
- It is very windy, with a high mean wind speed of 10–15 knots in most places. The frequent storms bring high sustained wind speeds and very high gusts, especially in the winter.

THE CHANGING CLIMATE

Most of the long running meteorological stations on the Antarctic Peninsula were established during the International Geophysical Year of 1957–58 and so have a climate record of over half a century for measuring changes. These have been remarkable, for example, the annual average temperature at Vernadsky Station (formerly Faraday) in the Argentine Islands rose by 3°C in the second half of the twentieth century. Whilst there are inter-annual variations, mainly driven by the presence or absence of sea ice during the winter, it is clear that the temperatures experienced on the Antarctic Peninsula in recent decades have been higher than the norm in recent centuries. The causes and evidence for the recent changes and their impacts on the Antarctic Peninsula Ice Sheet and the ecological systems of the region are discussed in detail in the chapter A Land of Change, p. 92.

OZONE AND THE OZONE HOLE

Ozone is a gas formed from three oxygen atoms. It is naturally created by the action of sunlight on the oxygen gas that we breathe. It is found throughout the atmosphere but has its highest concentration between 12 and 35 km (7 and 22 miles) altitude

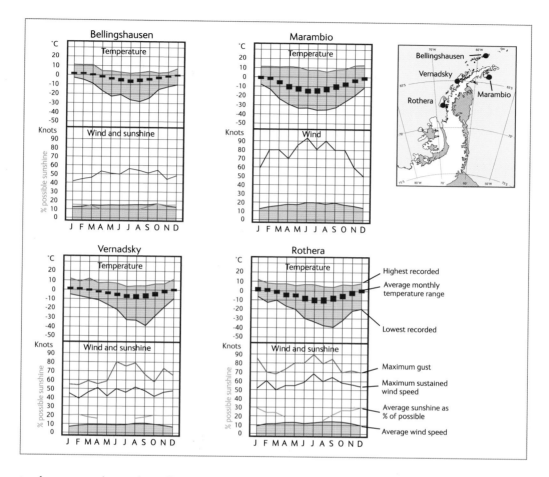

in the stratosphere, though even here it is not abundant. If all the ozone in a column to the top of the atmosphere was brought to ground level it would form a layer just three millimetres thick, but it is very important because it screens out harmful short-wavelength ultra-violet radiation in the sun's light which would otherwise be damaging to life, including humans.

The ozone hole occurs over Antarctica because here the stratosphere is sufficiently cold and stable during the winter for clouds to form in it. These clouds, known as polar stratospheric clouds, or more evocatively as nacreous or 'mother of pearl' clouds, form in the centre of the ozone layer, at heights between about 14 and 20 km (9 and 12 miles), when the temperature is below about -78°C (-108°F).

Summer visitors are unlikely to see these clouds because they are usually gone by October.

Chemical reactions take place on the surface of the clouds, which turn chlorine and bromine from ozone-depleting substances into an active form. Man-made chemicals such as early refrigerants, air-conditioning coolants, aerosol can propellants and halon fire-suppressants were a major source of this chlorine and bromine.

When the sun comes back in the Antarctic spring, photo-catalytic reactions take place which break down the ozone at the centre of the ozone layer back into oxygen at the rate of about 1% per day. By the time the hole is at its largest, virtually all the ozone at the centre of the ozone layer has gone. As the stratosphere warms up in the spring, the clouds disappear and ozone depletion ceases. Ozone rich air from outside the Antarctic eventually fills in the ozone hole, until the process starts again the following winter.

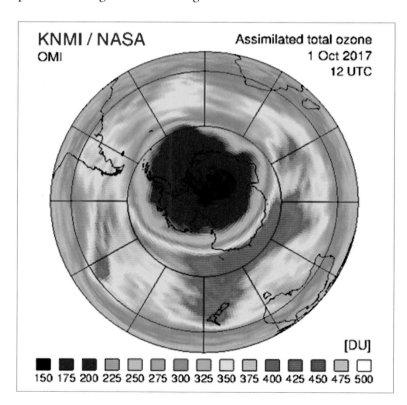

RIGHT
The ozone hole at its maximum extent in 2017 as shown by satellite observations. The centre of the hole is offset from the Pole towards the Atlantic.

Ozone depletion also occurs in the Arctic, but because the Arctic ozone layer is normally warmer than that of the Antarctic and ozone amounts start at a higher level than in the Antarctic, the threshold for a hole is harder to reach.

The Antarctic Peninsula lies near the edge of the ozone hole, which begins to form during the Antarctic winter. It is at its largest and deepest in early October, but is declining by the time the Antarctic summer season begins in November. It often persists into December, sometimes lasting until the summer solstice. This thinning of the ozone layer presents a significant hazard for the early season visitor, because substantially more ultra-violet light comes through the atmosphere when it is around, and Antarctic travellers have been sun-burnt in as little as five minutes.

Ozone amounts are measured at several Antarctic Peninsula research stations. In some places balloons are launched which carry sensors that measure ozone amounts in situ and draw a profile of the ozone layer from the ground to altitudes above 30 km (19 miles).

BELOW
Meteorologist Alex Grievson launching a balloon carrying ozone sensors at Rothera Research Station, Adelaide Island. The mountains of Graham Land are in the background.

ABOVE
Alpenglow on the mountains of the Antarctic Peninsula.

Other stations have spectrometers that measure the total ozone column from the ground. These observe sunlight coming through the atmosphere and measure how much absorption due to ozone takes place. Scientists at the British Antarctic Survey discovered the ozone hole in 1985. This discovery, and the realisation of its potential impact, led to the Montreal Protocol, which prohibits the release of ozone-depleting chemicals into the atmosphere. This international agreement has now been signed by all the UN Member States and is working well. Monitoring of these chemicals shows that their concentration in the atmosphere is going down. However they are so stable that it will be around 2075 before the concentration drops below that seen when the ozone hole first became detectable.

Light and darkness

There are many effects that change the appearance of the sky. First there are the changes associated with the seasons and latitude. It is often a pleasant shock for the traveller from the Northern Hemisphere to leave the northern winter and arrive in the southern summer. Many people are affected by the intensity of daylight and the low light of the northern winter gives rise to Seasonal Affective Disorder (SAD), which is dispelled by the bright summer sun. Heading further south the nights get steadily shorter. South of 54° is the land of simmer dim, where there is no true darkness after sunset (defined here as the sun being more than 12° below the horizon), only a period of twilight before the sun rises again. South of 60° there is a period of civil twilight, when the sky remains bright enough to read a newspaper at midnight. Crossing the Antarctic Circle at 66°34' south you enter the zone where at mid-summer the sun never sets, and at mid-winter never rises. This is actually reached a little further north as atmospheric refraction puts the sun a little higher in the sky than pure geometry predicts, and the sun is a disc not a point. The number of days with continuous sunlight or darkness increases by about six days per degree of latitude further south.

As the sun sets the sky undergoes subtle changes in colour. The mountain snows may show alpenglow, caused by the longer wavelength, redder parts of the spectrum being all that is left after the sunlight has made its long tangential passage through the Earth's atmosphere. Clouds may turn vivid pinks and reds, whilst in the opposite direction are the twilight colours, with their subtle shades of purple, blue and pink. After a major volcanic eruption these twilight colours are often enhanced, and at the same time alpenglow effects are much reduced because the light is absorbed by the volcanic aerosol.

BELOW
The midnight sun over Jenny Island and the southern tip of Adelaide Island, Marguerite Bay.

THE NIGHT SKY

Towards the end of summer it may get dark enough to see the southern night sky. If the night is clear, a visitor may be lucky enough to see the aurora australis (or the southern lights), though not all displays are spectacular. Most displays that are likely to be visible from the Antarctic Peninsula take the form of a faint glow low towards the southern horizon, occasionally becoming a little higher and showing green or red colouration. Rarer displays will show the full range of auroral features such as rays, curtains or an overhead corona.

The unpolluted air and absence of artificial light means that the Antarctic Peninsula is an exceptional place for stargazing. The Milky Way arches across the sky, incorporating the Southern Cross high in the south-east. The Magellanic Clouds are nearly overhead. They look almost like real clouds, faintly lit by light pollution, but in reality are smaller galaxies orbiting our own Milky Way. To the north lies Orion the hunter, but upside down to northern hemisphere observers.

LEFT
Aurora australis – waves and curtains of light in the night sky.

DAVID VAUGHAN

THE ICE SHEET

FOR THE GLACIOLOGIST, the Antarctic Peninsula represents a unique glacial environment, shaped by millennia of glacial flow, where recent, rapid climate warming has driven dramatic changes that are unprecedented within recent geological time. For the Antarctic traveller and photographer it represents an unparalleled meeting of ice and water; where light of unrivalled intensity plays on ice and ocean to create an unending palette – the burning glare of pure white snow only emphasising the inky depths of the nearby sea. Everywhere ice dominates the view and the environment, it has shaped the landscape that it now buries, and holds within it secrets of the past and lessons for the future.

ABOVE
Whilst the Antarctic Peninsula is one of the rockiest parts of the continent, its landscape is still overwhelmingly ice-covered, as shown here on Adelaide Island.

The Antarctic Peninsula contains a greater proportion of ice-free areas than other parts of the continent, but the first-time visitor might be surprised that, even here, the landscape is so completely dominated by the presence of snow and ice. Looking from the deck of a ship, the view is often dominated by near-vertical ice-cliffs from which icebergs topple into the ocean, above are highly-fractured glaciers that can move at more than a metre (3 ft) per day. On days when the cloud-base lifts it may be possible to see, high in the distance, ice spilling off mountainous islands and even the central spine of the peninsula. Here the high rate of annual snowfall keeps all but the steepest rock walls, and the tops of the tallest mountains, covered. It is a point for debate as to how many separate glaciers the Antarctic Peninsula has, but it is certainly more than 300. It is the discrete nature of these glaciers, flowing between mountains and ridges, that differentiates the Antarctic Peninsula from the more uniform and featureless ice sheets that lie to the south.

How glaciers form

Snow that simply falls and rests, eventually melting where it has fallen is described as 'snow-cover'. Where the climate is sufficiently cold, and snowfall sufficiently heavy, each year's snow cover might not melt away. Here, snow builds up from year to year, especially in hollows on the shaded side of mountains, and eventually forms a glacier.

Newly fallen snow is mostly air and has a density of about 0.3–0.5 tonnes per cubic metre (water = 1). The trapped air scatters light, making the snow look white. As the snow thickens the weight of new layers above compresses the older snow beneath. Over a period of decades to centuries, the snow undergoes a transformation into pure clear glacier ice.

The older snow first becomes packed into rounded grains like sugar, but over a few years of increasing compression as more snow falls above, the grains fuse together and the air spaces between the grains become smaller. This intermediate stage between snow and ice is called firn, or névé, and the density is now about 0.6 t/m^3.

Deeper still, the pressure becomes even greater, and the crystals crush together, further reducing space for air, until at about 70 m depth where the density is about 0.8 t/m^3, 'pore close off' is reached when air is finally trapped in isolated bubbles. At about 300–350 m, the final transformation occurs with the pressure in the ice becoming so great that the air in the bubbles is forced into the matrix of the ice and the ice becomes clear, and it can now have a density of about 90% of that of water. At this point, the gas still exists in the ice, and can be released by melting, often with an audible 'pop' as it is expelled under the same pressure at which it was captured.

BELOW
The transformation of snow to glacier ice.

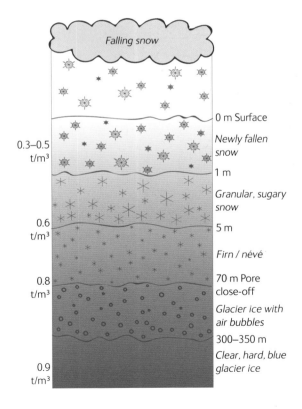

Falling snow

0.3–0.5 t/m³

0.6 t/m³

0.8 t/m³

0.9 t/m³

0 m Surface
Newly fallen snow
1 m
Granular, sugary snow
5 m
Firn / névé
70 m Pore close-off
Glacier ice with air bubbles
300–350 m
Clear, hard, blue glacier ice

On the northern Antarctic Peninsula, where there are several metres of snowfall per year and summer temperatures are close to 0°C, this whole process may take a few decades, but it takes many centuries in the continental interior where snowfall may be only centimetres per year, and the cold temperature means change is much slower.

The chemistry of the air trapped in the glacier ice contains vital details about the climate at the time the snow originally fell, including temperature and carbon dioxide levels. Scientists can reconstruct the evolution of the climate over time by extracting long ice cores from thick ice, that was built up from many centuries of snow fall, and analysing the trapped air (see p. 94).

RIGHT
Ice core extract from James Ross Island at 279 m depth. The central dark band is a volcanic ash layer that can help to confirm the age of the ice at this depth.

Glacier ice has large crystals and no longer has air bubbles that scatter light. This dense ice can absorb some red light and so the light that passes through it, or is reflected from the interior, tends to be at the blue end of the spectrum, giving glacier ice the bluish tint seen in icebergs and the sides of crevasses.

The workings of a glacier

A glacier is defined by glaciologists as a body of ice, in which the ice itself is moving from an area of accumulation to an area of loss (ablation). The newcomer to the polar regions may be most familiar with alpine glacier systems, such as the European Alps or the Rockies, which are dominated by land-terminating glaciers. In these glaciers, snow accumulates at high altitude where temperatures are cold enough for winter snowfall to survive the summer. Year-by-year, that snow will be buried by new snow, until, under the influence of gravity, it moves down the mountain to lower elevations. Here the summer temperatures will be significantly higher, sufficient that the ice melts and leaves the glacier in streams and rivers. In these alpine regions, the equilibrium line separates these two distinct zones of accumulation and ablation, and in summer this is marked by a transition between snow-covered areas and exposed ice.

Only a few glaciers in the extreme north of the Antarctic Peninsula and on some outlying islands, notably James Ross Island, have the same land-terminating configuration, the vast majority are marine-terminating. This situation arises because the climate is sufficiently cold that the equilibrium line sits at sea-level. Thus, throughout the year, snow can cover Antarctic Peninsula glaciers right down to sea-level. Although there are sometimes melt-water streams, and the occasional waterfall running into the sea in high-summer, for the most part, the loss of ice and snow from the glacier occurs by the calving of icebergs and direct melt of ice into the sea (see p. 56).

However, exactly the same as alpine glaciers, the glaciers on the Antarctic Peninsula are in a constant state of downhill movement. This occurs by two processes, the deformation of the ice itself and the movement of ice over its bed. The deformation occurs because when ice is subject to the intense forces produced within the glacier it can actually flow – rather like a very stiff syrup. This flow is, of course, too slow to see with the naked eye, but can often be seen in the apparently fluid shapes traced out on the surfaces of glaciers. The movement of ice over its bed, occurs either because the ice slides over the bed, or the bed itself deforms.

In either case, the movement is lubricated by the presence of water at the ice-rock interface. Some of this water begins as surface melt that finds its way to the bed through cracks and channels, but much is formed at the bed by friction and geothermal heat rising from deep in the Earth. The fact that most glaciers on the Antarctic Peninsula do not change their speed significantly from summer to winter, indicates

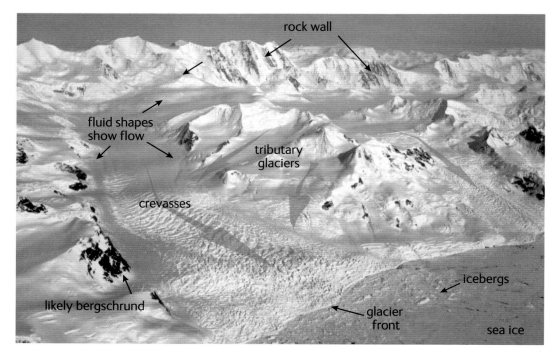

rock wall

fluid shapes
show flow

tributary
glaciers

crevasses

icebergs

likely bergschrund

glacier
front

sea ice

ABOVE
Typical features of an Antarctic
Peninsula glacier.

that the latter contribution is actually the more important. This water eventually finds its way to the glacier front and emerges into the sea. It is usually carrying sediment created by the grinding action of the glacier moving over its bed and appears as a milky plume that can extend a few hundred metres from the glacier front until it disperses.

A further consequence of the movement of ice is that glaciers evolve towards a natural state of equilibrium, where the mass of accumulated snow is balanced by the mass of snow transported downwards by glacier flow, and this in turn is balanced by the amount of ice lost back to the ocean. Several natural feedback processes work to keep this system in balance, with the result that the mass of ice contained in the volume of glaciers tends to remain constant in time, unless it is disrupted by some external influence such as a change in the climate or the amount of snowfall. In recent decades climate warming of up to 3°C (5.4°F) along the Antarctic Peninsula (see p. 45) has driven changes in the glaciers in the region; the large majority have retreated since the 1950s and the rate of flow has increased (see p. 96).

A few outlying islands around the north of the Antarctic Peninsula have areas that are free of permanent ice and have only a seasonal covering of snow. In some areas, for example Deception Island which is volcanically active and has areas of heated ground, this lack of glacial cover can be explained relatively easily, but in others, the reasons are not so obvious. Seymour Island is largely ice-free, but its near neighbour, Snow Hill Island, is covered by a significant ice cap. This apparent paradox may be an example of the significance of two-way interaction of ice and climate. While cold local climate is an obvious prerequisite for the survival of a glacier, the glacier itself will also modify that local climate. The presence of ice reflects a substantial amount of the sun's heat back into space, and the insulating effect of the snow prevents the rock beneath the ice absorbing heat in the summer and releasing it in the winter. Effectively, an ice-covered area will require a significant climate warming before the ice-cover is lost, but once the ice is gone it may require a substantial cooling before it returns.

CREVASSES AND CREVASSING

As a glacier flows, the ice within it is forced to deform, and this creates tremendous forces in the ice. These forces compress, stretch and shear the ice, but where they exceed the intrinsic strength of the ice, tearing can also occur. The voids opened up by this tearing are known as crevasses (see opposite).

Crevasses range in size from those that might easily be spanned by a single stride, to those tens of metres wide and with depths sometimes in excess of 100 m (328 ft). Two factors make crevasses a lethal hazard and even highly experienced Antarctic travellers have suffered falls into crevasses. Firstly, crevasses tend to occur in areas of rapid ice flow, often but not exclusively on steep slopes, or where the glacier changes its direction (see opposite). Once formed, they can be transported great distances before they eventually close, so that even for an expert, predicting the location of a crevasse is an inexact art. Secondly, after a crevasse has been formed, new snowfall can accumulate to form a snow-bridge over it, obscuring its location, and only sometimes providing a safe way across. A particularly dangerous type of crevasse is the bergschrund, which forms between ice and rock, and often

ABOVE AND RIGHT
Although equipment and clothing has improved considerably since these two photographs were taken in the 1950s, the necessity for training in crevasse rescue techniques has not diminished.

makes it difficult for geologists and climbers to access rock outcrops. Crevasse safety begins with avoidance, and travel within suspected crevassed areas should only be undertaken when absolutely necessary, even with special equipment.

Ice shelves

Where a glacier manages to flow off the land, and begins to float without either melting or breaking up into icebergs, it forms an ice shelf. A few rather small ice shelves exist in the Arctic mainly off the north coast of the Canadian Archipelago, but they are common in Antarctica and fringe most of the Antarctic coastline. The largest, the Ross Ice Shelf, is larger in area than Spain, and the thickest, the Ronne-Filchner Ice Shelf, is more than 3 km (1¾ miles) thick. The only area where ice shelves are not seen occupying bays around Antarctica is the north-west portion of the Antarctic Peninsula.

Recently, scientists have explained the absence of ice shelves here by a 'climatic limit of viability' that broadly corresponds to the -9°C (16°F) mean (average) annual air temperature (see p. 42). Weather and climate chapter). North of this boundary they do not survive and

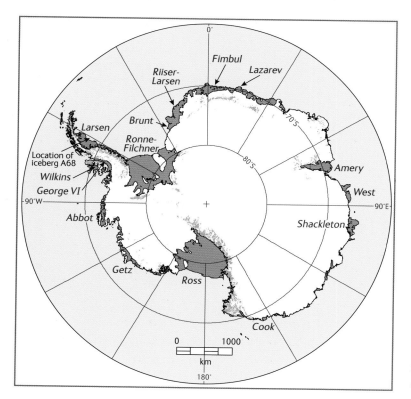

LEFT
Ice shelves fringe most of the Antarctic coastline.

RIGHT
Larsen C Ice Shelf after calving
of iceberg A68 in July 2017.
The background image is
a European Space Agency
Copernicus Programme
Sentinel-1 satellite radar image
from 28 August 2018 – in
the Antarctic winter. Satellite
radar imagery is invaluable
for monitoring changes in ice
shelves because it is unaffected
by darkness in the winter
months or cloud cover.

RIGHT
Larsen C Ice Shelf after calving
of iceberg A68 in July 2017.
The background image is
a European Space Agency
Copernicus Programme
Sentinel-1 satellite radar image
from 28 August 2018 – in
the Antarctic winter. Satellite
radar imagery is invaluable
for monitoring changes in ice
shelves because it is unaffected
by darkness in the winter
months or cloud cover.

in recent decades, as the regional climate has warmed, this limit has moved south with dramatic effects (see p. 98).

Driven by the continued flow of glaciers draining the ice off the continent, the ice shelf flows out further and further from the grounding line – perversely, the location where the glacier leaves the continent and starts to float. Eventually the ice shelf can grow so far out into the ocean that it becomes unstable and vulnerable to large icebergs calving off. This cyclical behaviour is normal for Antarctic ice shelves and different from ice shelf breakup related to regional climate change. There are many recorded examples, including the calving of iceberg A68 from Larsen C Ice Shelf in July 2017. This huge iceberg was one of the largest ever recorded and had an area of 5,800 km² – about the size of the US state of Delaware, or a quarter of the size of Wales reducing the area of the Larsen Ice Shelf by about 12%.

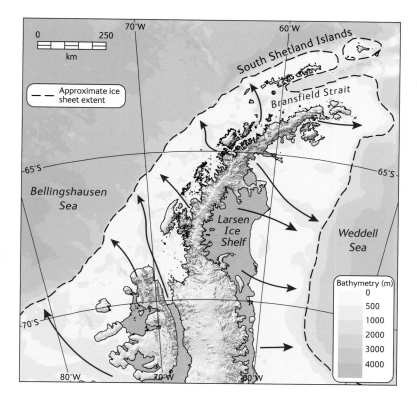

THE ANTARCTIC PENINSULA ICE SHEET SINCE THE LAST GLACIAL MAXIMUM AND THE ORIGIN OF FJORDS

The ice sheet on the Antarctic Peninsula today is only a small fraction of its former size during the Last Glacial Maximum, about 20,000 years ago. At that time grounded ice extended to the continental shelf edge on both sides of the Peninsula. Fast-flowing ice streams up to 40 km (24¾ miles) wide, similar to ones in other parts of Antarctica today, delivered large volumes of ice and sediment produced by glacial erosion to the continental margin.

Erosion beneath the ice streams over many glacial periods spanning millions of years carved broad troughs across the continental shelf and these are now prominent in bathymetric charts. Ice retreated from the continental shelves as temperatures increased and sea level rose during the Earth's transition out of the last glacial period. The main phase

RIGHT
Fast flowing ice streams carved
the deep channels seen in
bathymetric charts today.

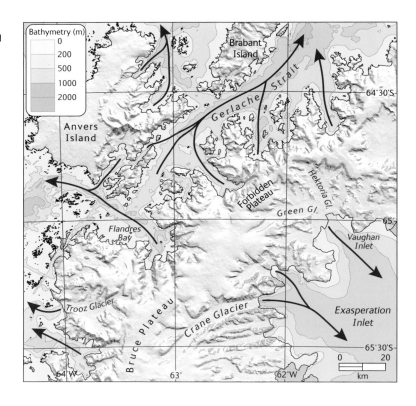

of retreat took place between 15,000 and 10,000 years ago, and in most areas the ice sheet margin had retreated close to its present-day position by 7,000 years ago. In some areas ice retreated a little beyond its present-day limits and the ice shelves in Prince Gustav Channel, Larsen A inlet and at least the northern part of George VI Sound collapsed and reformed long before the era of human exploration.

Today, detailed bathymetric surveys using advanced sonar systems reveal a landscape on the sea bed in fjords and further offshore that has been shaped by glacial erosion and deposition. Much of the erosion that carved the fjords along the Antarctic Peninsula probably occurred during phases of ice sheet advance and retreat, as at these times they contained fast-flowing, wet-based outlet glaciers. At times of maximum ice extent the fjords and the intervening headlands were completely buried by a thick, slow-flowing ice sheet that would have been frozen to its bed, resulting in relatively slow rates of erosion.

THE CHANGING ICE SHEET

Although, as mentioned, glaciers naturally reach equilibrium with the climate, when climate change occurs they must readjust to find a new equilibrium. We have already seen how the extent of the Antarctic Peninsula Ice Sheet was far greater in the much colder climate of 20,000 years ago. In recent decades, climate warming of up to 3°C (5.4°F) along the Antarctic Peninsula (see p. 45) has driven changes in both the glaciers and ice shelves. These phenomena are discussed in detail in the chapter A Land of Change, p. 92.

In order to understand the evolution of the glaciers and ice shelves and predict future change, we need to be able to measure past changes accurately. This is difficult for the vast and rarely visited Antarctic Peninsula, where past observations of glacier and ice shelf extents are sparse. Fortunately, aerial photography campaigns in 1947, 1956–58 and the late 1960s by UK and US agencies gained coverage of large parts of the northern Antarctic Peninsula. These were followed by the era of systematic satellite observations from the early 1970s to the present day, with increasing resolution and frequency of coverage. The British Antarctic Survey and Royal Navy have continued collecting aerial photographs of key areas since. The 70-year archive of photographs and satellite images is now an invaluable resource for scientists measuring and interpreting changes in the Antarctic Peninsula Ice Sheet.

BELOW
A US Navy aerial mapping photograph (left) and close-up (right) records the extent of the McMorrin Glacier, Graham Land, in February 1969 and are a valuable resource for measuring change.

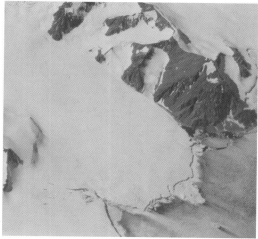

JON SHANKLIN

ICEBERGS AND SEA ICE

THE FIRST SIGHT OF ICE ON a voyage south is always exciting.
Edmond Halley wrote in his log on 1 February 1700, when at latitude
52° 24' S in the South Atlantic on an expedition to measure the
Earth's magnetic field, that: *'he fell in with great Islands of Ice, of Soe
Incredible a hight and Magnitude that I scarce dare to write my thoughts
of it.'* These 'islands' were the remains of a tabular iceberg that had
broken from an Antarctic ice shelf, and in those days encountering ice
at sea in a wooden ship would have been an alarming experience. The
visitor can still expect to see these harbingers of the frozen continent
on a crossing of the Drake Passage, but now from the safety of an ice-
strengthened and radar-equipped ship.

   Ice at sea is divided into two sorts: land ice, which was originally
formed from snow, has flowed to the sea as glacier ice, and eventually
broken away to form icebergs, and sea ice which was formed directly
from frozen sea-water.

Icebergs

Icebergs come in all shapes, sizes and colours, ranging from giant
flat-topped tabular icebergs that can be many kilometres in length,
through to small 'bergy-bits' 5–15 m (16–47 ft) long and 'growlers'

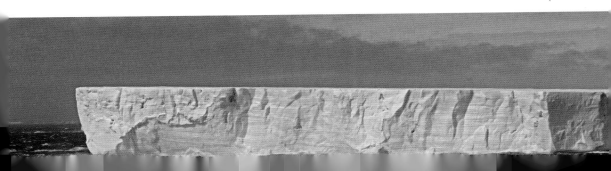

just 1–5 m (3–16 ft) long. Recently formed bergs show sharp features such as corners and towers, but as they melt and overturn they become smoothly sculpted. Older icebergs often have arches, shallow turquoise lagoons and elaborate fluting on their sides. Colours range from the white of the covering snow, through pastel shades of translucent blue ice into the indigo of deep, dark crevasses or submerged keels.

These icebergs originate from the glaciers and ice shelves that surround Antarctica by a process known as calving. Glaciers on the northern Antarctic Peninsula can be flowing at up to 1 m (3 ft) per day and they nearly all reach the sea. At the glacier front the constant downhill movement of the ice leads to a frequent fracturing of small icebergs into the sea, accompanied by a rumble as the ice slides into the sea and a sudden wave as the newly-born iceberg finds its level.

On occasion ice can melt and re-freeze at the bottom of a glacier, and when such ice calves off it gives rise to 'black' bergs, which lack the normal tiny bubbles of air which give the iceberg its white colour. Some icebergs that have originated from ice at the edge or middle of a glacier may incorporate part of the glacier's lateral or medial moraine, and will be impregnated with the boulders and rock debris accumulated by the glacier on its journey to the sea.

Calving from the ice fronts of ice shelves can take place at two speeds. The most common is a frequent fragmenting of many 'small' icebergs, usually less than 1,000 m (just over 1,000 yards) across. Occasionally giant icebergs tens of kilometres across can detach. Although these form much more rarely, they may contribute to the major loss of ice from a floating ice shelf. In the main, ice shelves give birth to flat-topped 'tabular' icebergs, whilst glaciers give rise to much more irregular bergs.

On the northern Antarctic Peninsula the significant ice shelves are on the east coast, and the Larsen Ice Shelf has seen several major collapses

BELOW
This tabular iceberg is probably about 2 km (just over 1 mile) long, with a freeboard of about 50 m (164 ft).

b

a

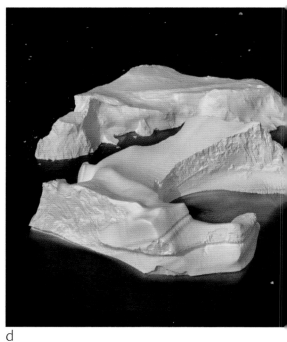

c   d

ABOVE
Several smaller icebergs with
towers, pinnacles, prows and
lagoons. (a), (b) and (c) are a
few tens of metres wide but (d)
is probably more than 100 m
(330 ft) long with a freeboard
of about 15 m (50 ft).

in the last few decades. First the most northerly part between Seal Nunataks and Cape Longing, called the Larsen A, broke apart in 1994, followed by the Larsen B south of Seal Nunataks to Jason Peninsula in 2002. (These events are described in more detail in the chapter A Land of Change, p. 99.) They did not result in giant tabular icebergs because these ice shelves were constrained in bays between prominent headlands, and the stress patterns within them produced many long and relatively thin icebergs instead, which dispersed quickly. In 2017 a 5,800 km² (2,239 miles²) section broke free from the Larsen C Ice Shelf in the form of a tabular iceberg designated as A-68 (see map p. 60).

Icebergs more than 16 km (10 nautical miles) across are given an identification letter and number by the US National Ice Center and are tracked on satellite imagery until they shrink below this limit. The letter defines the quadrant in which they originated and those from the Bellingshausen and Weddell Sea sector between 0° and 90°W are prefixed by A, whilst those from the other quadrants are prefixed anti-clockwise by B, C and D. The number is just a serial number for each quadrant, and to date a total of around 140 bergs have been numbered. Some of these tabular icebergs can be truly enormous. The largest iceberg tracked was called B-15 and broke off the Ross Ice Shelf, on the opposite side of the continent from the Antarctic Peninsula, in March 2000. It measured 295 km long and 37 km wide (183 and 23 miles), and had an area of about 11,000 km² (4,250 miles²), which is equivalent to that of Jamaica, or the English counties of Devon and Cornwall combined.

These giant icebergs can persist for several years, and travel great distances around the continent, drifting in the winds and currents that run along the coast in a predominantly anticlockwise direction. The tabular icebergs that are seen off the Antarctic Peninsula have come from the southern part of the Larsen Ice Shelf, the Ronne-Filchner Ice Shelf, or from ice shelves even further away, and have drifted round the continent.

The Weddell Sea gyre, (a current that rotates clockwise in the Weddell Sea), tends to push the majority of large icebergs that originate from the Larsen or Ronne-Filchner ice shelves north through a relatively narrow region about 100 km (60 miles) across

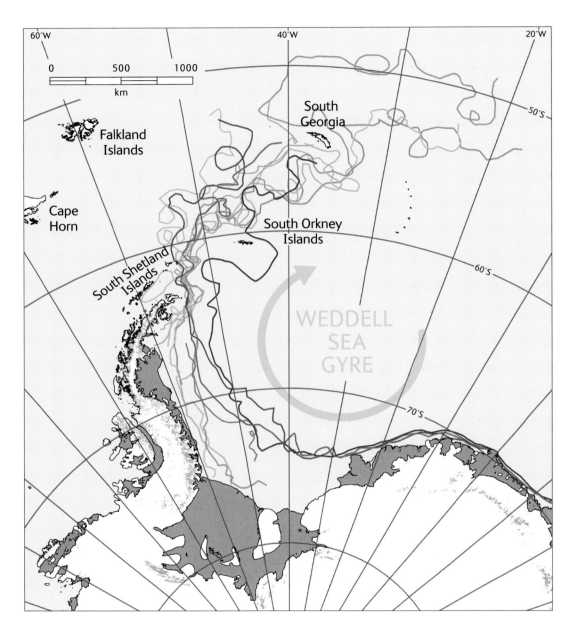

ABOVE
The tracks of large icebergs in
the Antarctic Peninsula region.

between the South Shetland Islands and the South Orkney Islands. Some run aground near the South Orkney Islands, but others drift into the South Atlantic where they may be seen on a crossing from South America or the Falkland Islands. The furthest north an iceberg is known to have survived was one logged by the *Dochra* on April 30 1894 at 26° 30' S, 25° 40' W, in the mid-Atlantic, at the latitude of southern Brazil. The map opposite plots the journeys of some of these behemoths.

Large icebergs are easy to see on a ship's radar, and are not much of a hazard for shipping. Ships should not approach too close however, as they often have hidden underwater keels and are also liable to turn turtle at any time. The major hazard is actually the eroded remains of these bergs in the form of 'bergy-bits' and 'growlers', which lie close to the water line and are difficult to spot in a swell. Even a small growler a metre across can do tremendous damage to a vessel if it strikes at speed, so a good look-out is essential in waters that are known to have icebergs. Sometimes even smaller fragments, less than 1 m (3 ft) across can do damage, as they are often herded together by wind and currents in the form of brash ice, which can have the same effect when hit at speed. If you are in a small boat with the engine switched off when

ABOVE
An armada of icebergs off the South Orkney Islands.

this brash ice is well spread-out and rocking slowly in a light swell you can hear the 'snap, crackle, pop' as the tiny high pressure air-bubbles trapped in the ice burst.

RIGHT
Typical winter and summer sea-ice extents. The north and west of the Antarctic Peninsula usually becomes ice free during the summer, allowing ships to venture along the coast.

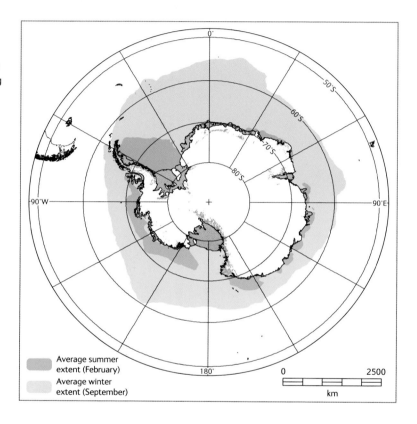

Average summer extent (February)
Average winter extent (September)

Sea ice

The winter formation of sea ice round Antarctica virtually doubles the size of the continent and is one of the Earth's great seasonal transformations.

Ice begins to form in salt water when its temperature drops below -1.8°C (29°F) and first appears as an oily film on the sea surface known as 'grease-ice'. If there is a little wind to generate a swell this ice can break up, and the resulting fragments become rounded with turned up edges where they rub together, forming 'pancake' ice.

As more ice forms the wind drives the individual floes together to form a continuous mass of individually moving ice floes called pack ice. Where the pack becomes tightly compressed the individual floes can coalesce to form a continuous sheet called an ice field. In the 1950s and 1960s, surveyors and geologists carrying out exploratory surveys by long dog-sledging journeys relied on this continuous sea ice to gain access to offshore islands. This could be extremely dangerous and there were several deaths and near-misses when the ice suddenly started to break up, or areas of thin, weak ice were encountered unexpectedly.

As the ice thickens further it excretes salt back into the sea, slowly becoming fresher and harder. Eventually, at the end of winter, its thickness can reach 1–2 m (3–6 ft) and although most will break up and

BELOW
Pancake ice, with icebergs and sunset. The pinnacle seen on the left of the photograph is connected to the main iceberg by a submerged keel not far below the surface.

RIGHT
The ice-strengthened *RRS Ernest Shackleton* making its way through pack ice in the Weddell Sea.

RIGHT
Pack ice stretching to the horizon in the Bellingshausen Sea.

melt over the summer, a few floes survive, particularly in the Weddell Sea. These can become thicker in succeeding winters, but reach a limit of 3–4 m (9–12 ft) as sub-surface melting balances surface accumulation of snow. On a temporary basis, rafting during gales creates hummocks and bummocks, much thicker areas above and below the surface.

On the west coast of the Antarctic Peninsula the pack ice is usually relatively light, but its extent can vary dramatically from one year to the next. In part this is what gives rise to the large variation in mean temperature at some of the Antarctic Peninsula weather stations, described on pp. 42–44. In years when there is little pack ice the air temperature is not far from the freezing temperature of sea-water, but in years when there is a vast expanse of field ice the climate becomes much more continental with considerably lower winter temperatures.

Ships operating in Antarctic waters must be designed to cope with encountering at least one-year old sea ice. Ice-strengthened ships have a double hull that has a rounded bow made of thickened steel with extra stiffening, and is specially shaped to protect the propeller at the stern. They often have thrusters that allow manoeuvring in small areas of open water and backing up to allow ramming of the ice ahead. Most expedition tour ships and ships supplying Antarctic research stations are of this type.

Icebreakers have the extra characteristics of enormously powerful engines and a bow that is designed to ride up onto the ice surface so that the weight of the ship will then break the ice, allowing forward progress, even through thicker multi-year sea ice.

The pack ice is often in continual motion, driven by the wind and ocean currents, sometimes moving at several knots. Oppositely directed wind and current can create tightly packed floes which are difficult for even an ice-strengthened ship to break through due to the ice pressure. Ships now have access by satellite link to sophisticated information systems such as Polar View (www.polarview.aq) that give daily updates about sea ice density and distribution based on radar satellite imagery. These details, often along with reconnaissance imagery from drones operated from the ship, allow navigators to plot the best route through sea ice and avoid areas where the ship could become trapped.

A small change in wind can release the pressure and a stuck ship can resume its progress. Often when a ship is breaking through floes, they are overturned, revealing shades of pink, yellow, green or brown. This is not paint from the ship, but snow algae growing on the snow and underside of the ice. Broken multi-year ice can also show bands of diatoms which live on the underside of the floe and are encased in more ice each winter.

The fjords and channels along the coast can trap pack ice for much longer than in the open sea. Sometimes a thin skim of ice forms on these coastal waters, even though the temperature is too warm for sea ice to form. Melt-water from glaciers has created a thin surface layer of fresh-water, and this freezes much more easily due to its lower salinity.

BELOW
Typical early summer sea ice in Marguerite Bay, looking west towards Adelaide Island.

At the boundary between land or ice shelf and the pack covered sea, a region of fast-ice forms. This is sea ice several metres thick that is firmly attached and sometimes provides an easy route ashore. Emperor penguins often have their colonies on this ice, but on occasions when there is a wide stretch of open water in front of the fast-ice, swell can break off the ice and take the colony with it. Where fast-ice joins land, there is often a 'tide-crack' at the boundary, and when covered with snow this can be a hazard for the unwary.

Around Antarctica as a whole there has been little overall change in maximum sea ice amount over the last 40 years. This broad statement hides regional patterns and the Bellingshausen Sea, to the West of the Antarctic Peninsula, has generally seen a decline. The explanation is linked to the changes that we have contributed to the atmosphere, by creating the ozone hole and adding greenhouse gasses, as described on pp. 45 and 101. This has changed the atmospheric circulation around the continent, and with changes to the patterns of winds has come changes to the sea ice.

Daily satellite observations of sea-ice extent are available for around 40 years, providing researchers with a detailed record of regional trends and variations. Looking forward in time, it is likely that as the ozone hole becomes weaker, the total sea ice round Antarctica will decline. In 2017 there were record low amounts of sea ice around Antarctica, but it is too soon to say whether this represents a significant change in behaviour. Because sea ice and climate are interlinked, a reduction in sea-ice cover will lead to further, as yet unknown, consequences for the regional climate.

PETER CONVEY
LIFE ON LAND

THE POLAR REGIONS ARE CLEARLY challenging places to live in. Animals, plants and microbes that make it their home face low temperatures and high winds, solar radiation, freezing and desiccation, and often very low nutrient availability. Seasonal differences are extreme; beyond the polar circles, the sun remains below the horizon for days to months in winter, and above it in summer. In winter, terrestrial (land) habitats of both north and south poles face extremely low air temperatures, in coastal regions dropping regularly to -20 to -40°C, (-4 to -40° F) and down to -60°C (-76°F) or lower inland in Antarctica. However, the climatic isolation of the Antarctic continent by the Antarctic Convergence means that in the summer it faces considerably lower temperatures than the Arctic at equivalent latitudes. A further important contrast between the two polar regions is in the amount of land available for terrestrial organisms. The Antarctic is a large and ice-covered continent centred over the South Pole and surrounded and isolated by the vastness of the Southern Ocean, while the Arctic includes the northern regions of the European, Asian and North American continents, surrounding the Arctic Ocean.

BELOW
Typical Antarctic Peninsula scenery at Léonie Island, Marguerite Bay, showing the sparsity of suitable terrain for colonisation by vegetation and terrestrial animals.

The combination of these differences in geography, and the climatic differences they drive, means that less than 0.2% (or about 20,000 km²) of Antarctica's area is seasonally ice- and snow-free, while most of the great northern continental areas, apart from the Greenland Ice Sheet, are ice free in summer. Air temperature provides a poor measure of the actual temperatures that organisms face, because sunshine warms soil, rock surfaces and vegetation, while snow can provide an insulating blanket. The variation of temperature within Antarctic microhabitats on land can be surprisingly great, 20–30°C (68–86°F) within minutes or hours, and 40–60°C (104–140°F), even up to 100°C (212°F), over a full year.

As well as low and fluctuating temperatures, organisms living in Antarctica face many environmental challenges. The most important is access to liquid water, necessary to all life on Earth, but severely limited in Antarctica. Whilst parts of the Antarctic Peninsula receive up to 3,000 mm (120 in) of rain equivalent per year, this water remains frozen most of the time. Contrasting with the Peninsula, much of the interior of the Antarctic continent is a frigid desert with extremely low precipitation compounded by low levels of humidity, which can result in the formation and maintenance of relatively large ice-free areas in 'dry valleys', particularly well developed in parts of the Transantarctic Mountains.

Although the high latitude means that the sun is relatively low in the sky, during the summer months the long days mean that the amount of solar energy received at ground level can accumulate to give greater daily totals than at temperate latitudes. This can lead to greater plant productivity through photosynthesis, but it also has the potential to increase light stress. The high albedo (reflectance) of snow and ice can also add to the amount of solar radiation received on adjacent ice-free ground. However, in the northern Antarctic Peninsula region the typically cloudy conditions reduce the occurrence of extreme radiation stresses.

The annual formation of the ozone hole over Antarctica during spring, caused by anthropogenic pollutant gases released into the atmosphere, provides an additional potential stress for life, as it results in high levels of biologically damaging UV-B radiation reaching the ground – comparable to those normally experienced in midsummer – at a time of year when many organisms are still inactive. There was initially some concern that there would be drastic and harmful biological consequences, but studies carried out along the Antarctic Peninsula indicate that affected organisms are capable of responding and protecting themselves. While these responses are more subtle than initially expected, they still involve important changes in the way the organisms use available resources. Such information will be useful for scientists who are trying to understand responses to environmental change more widely in biological systems.

In recent decades parts of the Antarctic, particularly the Antarctic Peninsula and some of the sub-Antarctic islands of the Southern Ocean, have experienced some of the most rapid rates of environmental change on the planet. Their organisms and ecosystems are expected to be sensitive biological indicators of the consequences of environmental change, relevant not only to the polar regions, but to ecosystems and our ability to understand, predict and mitigate change globally.

Terrestrial habitats

Any exposed surface can, in principle, be colonised by organisms with suitable attributes. Rocks and very simple soil surfaces on even the most southerly nunataks on the Antarctic Peninsula are colonised by lichens, mosses, micro-organisms, and some invertebrate animals. At such locations, seasonal snow and ice cover can provide a buffer to the extreme thermal and radiation conditions. The summer warming of rock and soil surfaces leads to the melting of surrounding snow and ice on a very local scale, providing water for the organisms present. The length of time water is available varies between weeks and months each year at locations along the Antarctic Peninsula. Water can also penetrate the surface of some rocks, allowing microbial communities to develop there (known as endolithic microbes). These habitats appear to provide one of the limits to the life that occurs on Earth, and have been used as an analogy by those seeking to understand and predict how life might have evolved and survive on other worlds.

About 3% of the total area of the Antarctic Peninsula is ice free, compared to only 0.2% for the continent as a whole. Antarctic

Peninsula land habitats often consist simply of rock, boulder and rubble surfaces, the vast majority of which appears barren at first sight. The simple soils are generally little more than fragmented rock debris, and contain very low amounts of nutrients and carbon. Rock is fragmented by processes such as glacial action, water (particularly freeze-thaw cycles), salt weathering, insolation (heating) and wind action. Lichens also contribute to the erosion of rock surfaces. 'Brown' soils and peats, more familiar from lower latitudes, are found only in very small areas in Graham Land, the former associated with the very limited stands of the two flowering plants occurring there, although they are more widespread on the sub-Antarctic islands.

Unconsolidated rock debris and soils are usually too mobile to permit colonisation by plants. A permanently frozen layer called permafrost is typically found beneath Antarctic Peninsula soils, along with those of the South Shetland and South Orkney Islands, although this is not the case in the sub-Antarctic islands. While permafrost is not a habitat for an active biological community, the layer of wet soil that covers it (and only freezes in winter) does support biological communities. Soil mixing organisms, particularly earthworms, are not present on the Antarctic Peninsula or continent, but do occur in the sub-Antarctic.

Antarctic land habitats are often exposed to abrasion (damage by impact) by rock debris or snow and ice crystals, encouraged by the frequent high winds. Soil movement during freeze-thaw cycles also limits where vegetation can grow. Both established vegetation and the simple soil matrix support invertebrate and microbial communities, which otherwise tend to be limited to more protected habitats, such as in cracks in rocks and their undersurfaces. Where substrata are sufficiently stable, a vegetation community can develop. Rock surfaces are colonised by lichens, with crevices being occupied by algae and mosses. Microbial crusts stabilise soil surfaces, followed by moss and lichen communities. Rarely these may develop into deeper peat banks over centuries to millennia, which provide a valuable record of previous climates complementing those available from ice cores and sedimentary records. The best developed examples of these sensitive habitats are found in relatively inaccessible locations on Signy Island (South Orkney Islands), Elephant Island (South Shetland Islands), and Green Island (Berthelot

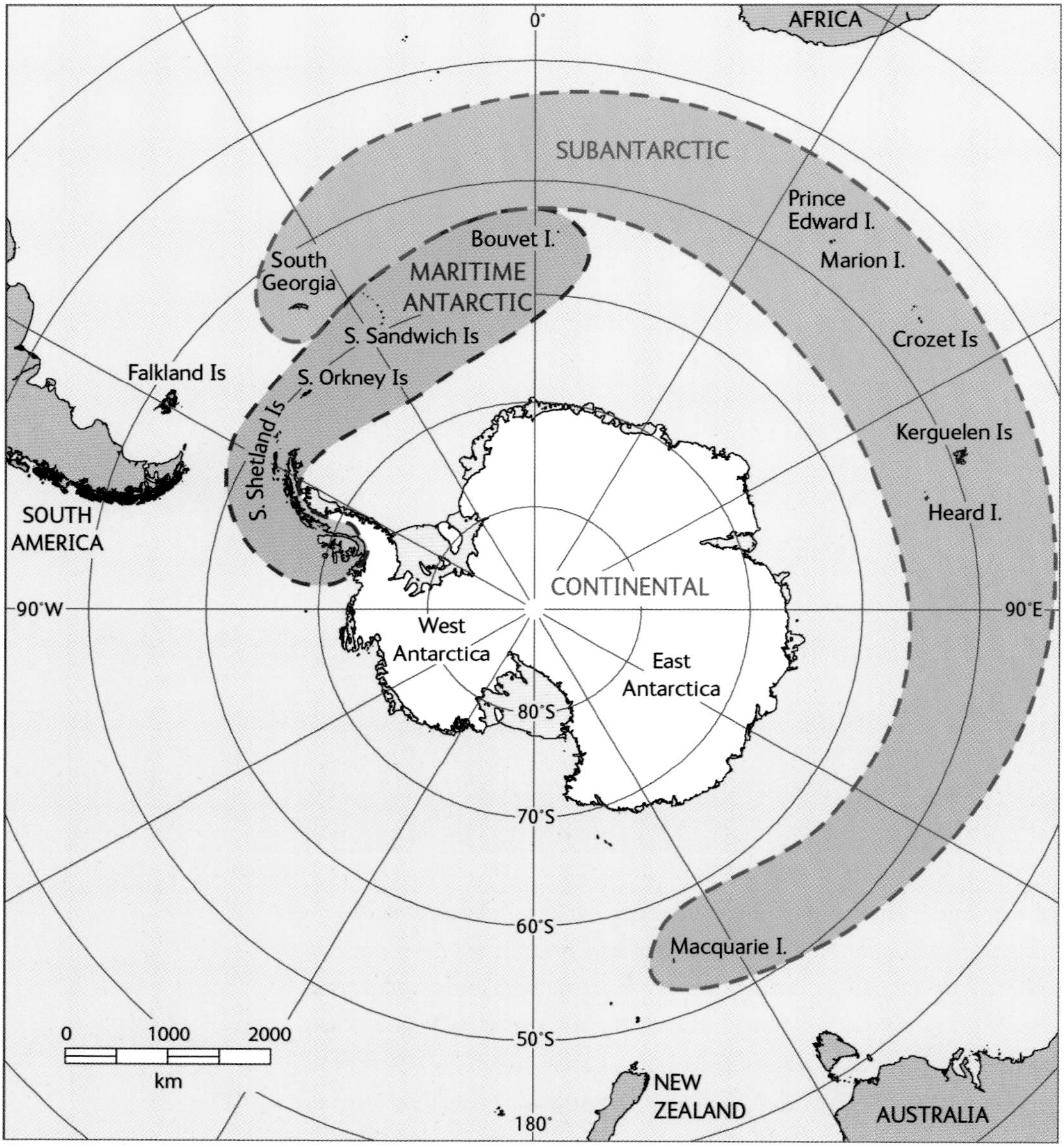

ABOVE
The Antarctic is often considered in three separate regional or biogeographical divisions: the sub-Antarctic, maritime and continental zones.

Islands). A number of the Antarctic Specially Protected Areas (ASPAs) in the Antarctic Peninsula region, including Green Island, have been so designated to provide protection to unusually well vegetated locations. However, many visitor sites have good examples of these typical moss and lichen dominated communities, which are often described as 'fellfield'.

Zones of life

Antarctica covers a very large area, about twice that of Australia, or 1.4 times the size of the USA. Within this area are found a wide range of ecosystems and organisms. For convenience, the Antarctic is often considered in three separate regional or biogeographic divisions: the sub-Antarctic, maritime and continental zones. These divisions are pragmatic and practically useful, although the true biogeographic complexity of Antarctica is much greater, with 16 distinct 'Antarctic Conservation Biogeographic Regions' (ACBRs) currently recognized within the continent. Most visits to the Antarctic are concentrated in the northern Antarctic Peninsula region (Graham Land), and also the associated archipelagos of the South Shetland Islands and South Orkney Islands. These lie within and are typical of the maritime Antarctic zone, and the descriptions following therefore focus on the terrestrial (land) life of this zone.

The maritime Antarctic, as its name suggests, is strongly influenced by its proximity to the ocean, especially during the summer months when the sea is largely free of ice. As a result, mean monthly air temperatures in summer are positive if low (1–4°C) (34–39°F), while the mean temperatures in winter, -10 to -15°C (14 to 5°F) are not as extreme as those faced in the continental interior. Seasonal snow cover is a feature of this region, covering most flatter ground other than exposed ridges and cliffs, and providing physical protection as well as maintaining temperatures at levels above the extreme lows experienced for short periods in the open in winter.

VEGETATION

The 'lower' plants – the mosses, liverworts and lichens – dominate maritime Antarctic vegetation, and there are approximately 100, 25 and

250 species, respectively. Occasionally, visible fungi (toadstools) will also be encountered. Vegetation is typically scattered with a few large continuous stands and patches separated by areas of bare ground and rock. Colonisation of newly available ground – for instance land that has been exposed by current and widespread glacial retreat – can be very rapid, with visible clumps appearing within years of ice retreat and more general ground coverage soon after. Although individual moss clumps are short-lived, some lichens are thought to be 300–600 years old. The few peat banks known from the maritime Antarctic have accumulated over the last 5,000–6,000 years.

Only two species of flowering plant occur naturally on the Antarctic continent, the grass *Deschampsia antarctica* and the pearlwort *Colobanthus quitensis*, both limited to the Antarctic Peninsula, South Shetland Islands and South Orkney Islands.

a

RIGHT AND OPPOSITE
Typical elements of the vegetation communities of the Antarctic Peninsula. (a) Carpets of the foliose alga, *Prasiola crispa*, develop in summer, often near to vertebrate sources of nutrients. (b) Clumps of the Antarctic hairgrass, *Deschampsia antarctica*, growing amongst the wet-ground moss, *Sanionia uncinata*, on Anchorage Island, Marguerite Bay. (c) Fruiting cushions of the Antarctic pearlwort, *Colobanthus quitensis*, along with small plants of *D. antarctica* at the species' most southern known location in the Antarctic on northern Alexander Island. (d) Peat bank representing over 5,000 years' accumulation on Signy Island, South Orkney Islands. (e) A typical open fellfield community of scattered mosses and lichens on a coastal rock exposure on Charcot Island. (f) Epilithic (rock surface) lichen communities are particularly well developed at locations on the Antarctic Peninsula, as illustrated by the large *Umbilicaria* thalli here.

This diversity is strikingly low in comparison with even the archipelagos of the High Arctic (Svalbard alone has more than 100 species of flowering plant) and indicates the importance of the physical isolation of the Antarctic, as well as its extreme conditions, in controlling the level of biodiversity found there. These two plants are, nevertheless, widely distributed throughout the maritime Antarctic, being found as far south as the northern tip of Alexander Island.

b

c

e

d

f

In a few locations in the South Orkney and South Shetland islands individual grass plants have coalesced to form extensive swards or lawns of several tens of square metres in extent. Smaller swards of several metres extent are found sporadically throughout the grass distribution along the Antarctic Peninsula, and even at its most southern known location. The grass almost always occurs alongside the pearlwort, although individual plants of the latter rarely coalesce to form larger stands. On the South Shetland Islands an unusual isolated grass 'hummock' growth form is also found on some raised beaches, with individual hummocks being 50 cm (20 in) or more in diameter. However, more typically, both the grass and the pearlwort are found as individual or small groups of plants, occurring from just above the shoreline to altitudes of 200–250 m (650–820 ft). Both species appear to be responding rapidly to the regional warming being experienced in the Antarctic Peninsula region, with population expansion of one to two orders of magnitude over as little as 30–50 years at the few monitored locations. Biological responses to climate change in the Antarctic Peninsula region are discussed further on p. 101.

Fellfield vegetation is very sensitive to disturbance through, for instance, trampling. Mosses and liverworts (and the lichens that often grow epiphytically on them) do not have roots like higher plants, and are therefore easily dislodged from the soil surface, whilst even lichens that are apparently very firmly attached to rocks are brittle and vulnerable to mechanical damage, particularly when dry. Even apparently bare soils are typically cemented together at the surface by a microbial crust, which is the first stage of community development in these ecosystems. Footprints and vehicle tracks left in moss and soil are often visible and largely unchanged several decades after their creation, illustrating the very slow recovery rates typical of these extremely sensitive habitats.

This highlights the importance of taking great care when walking on land in the Antarctic Peninsula region, and as far as possible avoiding walking on or otherwise disturbing the vulnerable moss and lichen vegetation, and even the soil surface. For this reason a number of visitor sites have designated walking routes or, in their absence, guidelines on appropriate walking behaviour, which should be followed.

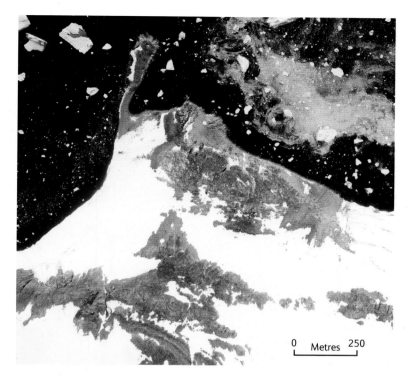

0   Metres   250

ANIMAL LIFE

There are no land or freshwater vertebrates on the Antarctic continent, although there are locally large breeding and resting/moulting concentrations of marine vertebrates including seals, penguins and other birds. These can fertilise and encourage the development of vegetation and associated invertebrate communities. The soil invertebrate fauna is patchily distributed and includes protozoa, tardigrades, rotifers, nematodes, enchytraeid worms, mites and collembolans (springtails).

All of these animals are small – the largest Antarctic Peninsula mites and springtails are only 1–2 mm ($\frac{1}{32}$–$\frac{1}{16}$ in) long, although they can easily be found in their thousands, and the other groups are largely microscopic. However, with a little effort, all can be found and seen easily with a hand lens. Freshwater invertebrates include a number of crustaceans, which can again be very abundant in both small melt pools and larger lakes.

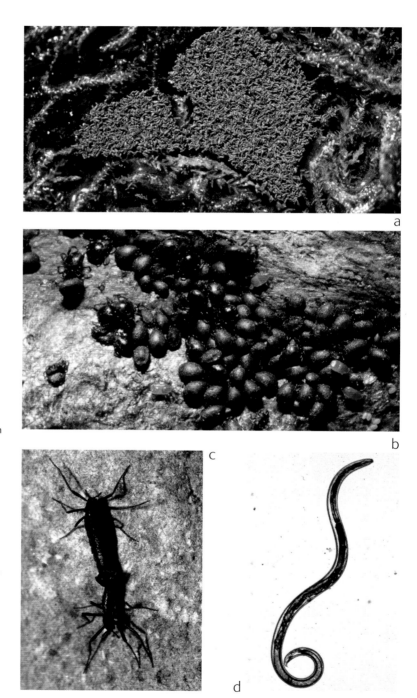

RIGHT
Examples of the terrestrial invertebrates that may be encountered in the Antarctic Peninsula region. (a) A raft of several thousand springtails, *Cryptopygus antarcticus*, temporarily trapped on a small water surface on moss. (b) The mite, *Alaskozetes antarcticus* (black), is one of the largest herbivores found on the Antarctic Peninsula – the elephant of the ecosystem! The smaller orange mite, *Gamasellus racovitzai*, is one of the few predators – the lion – whose diet mainly consists of springtails. (c) A mating pair of the endemic midge, *Belgica antarctica*; the species is wingless, but can form dense swarms on the ground much as its more familiar winged relatives do in the air. (d) Soil nematodes form an abundant and important element of the invertebrate community, but only the largest are visible to the naked eye.

There is a very low representation of 'higher' invertebrate groups, the maritime Antarctic hosting only two species of fly: *Belgica antarctica*, a wingless midge known only from the Antarctic Peninsula and South Shetland Islands, and *Parochlus steinenii*, Antarctica's only flying insect, a midge limited to the South Shetland Islands and South Georgia in the Antarctic region but also occurring in southern South America. Both are less than 0.5 cm (⅕ in) in length and are chironomid midges, representative of a global and very familiar family that includes the swarming midges of temperate and tropical latitudes.

Despite the small and apparently insignificant nature of these terrestrial invertebrate and plant communities, they provide extremely important tools for research. They contain all the major functional elements of the much more complex and visible communities with which we are more familiar (i.e. producers, grazers, predators, decomposers). Combined with their overall simplicity (low species diversity) and the lack of confounding human influences that are pervasive elsewhere, they provide ideal model systems to help us better understand how all ecosystems are structured and function. Furthermore, they are thought to be particularly sensitive and responsive to the different and complex elements of environmental change. This is happening more rapidly in the Antarctic Peninsula region than virtually anywhere else on the planet, and so these terrestrial ecosystems and their contained species are like the 'canary in the coalmine', helping us to better understand the likely wider consequences of change for ecosystems globally (see p. 101).

UNUSUAL ECOSYSTEMS

In addition to the typical terrestrial ecosystems described above, there are some more unusual ecosystems associated with the small number of geothermally active locations in the Antarctic, including features such as fumaroles, warmed ground, and heated pools or springs. In the Antarctic Peninsula region these are found only on Deception Island (S. Shetland Islands) where they receive strict protection from visitor impacts. The characteristics of the Deception Island volcano are described on pp. 28–29. Such features are also well developed on the remote and rarely visited S. Sandwich Islands, also within the maritime Antarctic. These locations provide warmth and liquid water, although they also have the stresses associated with chemical weathering and challenges such as high acidity, mineral and sulphur levels. They can host rich communities of mosses, liverworts and invertebrates otherwise unknown elsewhere in the region.

INTRODUCED SPECIES

Direct human contact with Antarctica has only happened over the last two centuries, and much of the region still remains relatively pristine and unimpacted, at least relative to other continents. However, human presence has inevitably resulted in the transfer of non-native organisms into the Antarctic. Currently, around 200 non-native species are known to be established in the wider Antarctic region, with approximately 95% of these occurring on the sub-Antarctic islands, and about half being flowering plants and a third being insects. These numbers are likely to be underestimates, and indicate the already considerable impact of human activity on biodiversity in parts of the Antarctic.

A small but increasing number of non-native species are currently known from the Antarctic Peninsula and Scotia Arc archipelagos, with the majority of these being present on the South Shetland Islands (one fly, 3–5 springtails and one grass) and South Orkney Islands (one fly and one enchytraeid worm). Fewer examples have been reported from the Antarctic Peninsula itself, although a springtail is known from as far south as Marguerite Bay, and two grasses between the tip of the Peninsula and the northern end of the Gerlache Strait. While individually these may seem insignificant, their potential importance to ecosystem function is amply demonstrated by the South Orkney Islands fly. In the relatively limited area where it currently occurs it reaches population densities high enough to far outweigh the decomposition activity of the entire native invertebrate community. An individual plant of the Tierra del Fuego species, *Nassauvia magellanica*, was removed as a potential alien in 2010, although this example also illustrates the difficulty of separating a natural colonist from a human-assisted alien when it is discovered some time after establishment, as is normally the case.

a

b

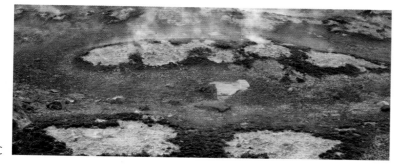

c

d

LEFT

Geothermally active sites, such as those on Deception Island and several of the South Sandwich Islands, host very unusual moss and liverwort communities that are exceptional in the entire Antarctic region. (a) Fumaroles and other geothermally active sites provide a permanent source of heat and water, allowing development of exceptional vegetation communities on otherwise barren ground. (b) Leafy liverworts and mosses, many of which occur at no other location in the Antarctic, growing around small vents in the soil surface emitting moist air at about 30°C (86°F). (c) Spectacularly zoned vegetation, indicating different thermal tolerances, around a much hotter series of vents on Bellingshausen Island (South Sandwich Islands); the bare ground in the centre of the patches is 70–90°C (158–194°F) at the surface, while temperatures of 40–45°C are found as little as 2 cm below the surface of the inner ring of *Campylopus* moss. (d) Lush mosses and liverworts growing around a large fumarole vent on Bellingshausen Island.

a

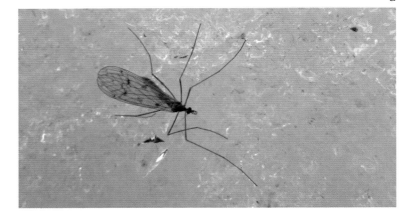

b

RIGHT
A small number of 'alien' invertebrate and plant species have already become established in the maritime Antarctic, where they have potential to introduce major changes in the function of ecosystems. (a) The chironomid midge, *Eretmoptera murphyi*, has been established on Signy Island since the late 1960s, and its distribution is currently expanding quite rapidly. (b) A trichocerid fly, *Trichocera maculipennis*, first recorded near a research station on King George Island in the mid 2000s, has become established; it is a northern boreal scavenging species with good pre-adaptation to the environmental conditions of the maritime Antarctic. (c) A single plant of *Nassauvia magellanica* that was found near Whalers Bay on Deception Island in 2009 had obviously been established for several years before its discovery and removal.

c

The adoption and utilisation of appropriate biosecurity procedures is now an urgent priority for national operators, non-governmental organisations and the tourist industry working in the Antarctic region. These can be simple, common sense and effective – for instance removing mud from boots and equipment, using disinfecting boot baths, and checking clothes, rucksacks and camera equipment for seeds, both before departure for the Antarctic and between landings at different sites within the region. As demonstrated by both older and very recent introductions of plants, beetles and flies to sub-Antarctic South Georgia, the primary and most effective control measure in reality must be the prevention of transfer. Many of the organisms that are most likely to become established are small and inconspicuous and often are unlikely to be spotted by anyone other than an expert, especially when present in very small initial numbers. Once established, such organisms will be virtually impossible to eradicate. Thus, the simple biosecurity measures practiced on many cruise vessels are not trivial or token efforts, but represent the main line of defense currently protecting Antarctic terrestrial ecosystems from biological invasions. Please adhere to them!

DAVID VAUGHAN

A LAND OF CHANGE

THE ANTARCTIC PENINSULA DIFFERS from the rest of the Antarctic continent in very many ways, but the key difference is in its climate. While on the rest of Antarctica temperatures are almost permanently below freezing, the Antarctic Peninsula has summer temperatures that are sometimes balmy in comparison. Here, melting snow and ice is widespread during the summer months and many coastal areas are ice-free, providing a rich habitat for plants and animals. The warmer parts of the peninsula have long been disparagingly referred to by those venturing further south as the 'banana belt'.

However, this has not always been the case. Throughout geological history, climate has changed. It has changed over millions of years as the continental plates drifted from equatorial regions towards the poles. On occasion it has changed rapidly as massive meteorites that hit the Earth threw great clouds of dust into the atmosphere, effectively shielding the surface from the Sun. Over the last million years, the planet has been through a succession of warm and cold phases in which the concentration of greenhouse gases (notably carbon dioxide and methane) in the atmosphere has risen and fallen. In the northern hemisphere, these so-called glacial/inter-glacial cycles saw the waxing and waning of massive ice sheets that covered North America, Siberia and Europe. These were so large that the water they took from the oceans caused sea levels to fall by more than 120 m (394 ft). In Antarctica, the ice sheet spread across the coastal seas to the edge of the continental shelves, then retreated again (see p. 61). As recently as 20,000 years ago, ice dominated north and south and the world was a very different place. As the ice sheet retreated, a process largely complete by 10,000 years before today, it left the landscape we know. Around the Antarctic Peninsula, even areas that are not today covered by ice bear the marks of it. Even below the waves, the direction of ancient ice flow is gouged into the seabed (see p. 62).

Today, the natural processes that caused the coming and going of ice across much of the planet have been outdone by a much stronger influence. In just 250 years, human activity has pushed greenhouse gases far beyond any natural change that occurred for at least a million years (see pp. 94–95). The future of the climate is now uncertain, but the scientific consensus is that temperatures are rising as a result of human emissions and even the world's greatest remaining wilderness will not escape.

In this chapter, we will consider the evidence for climate change on and around the Antarctic Peninsula, and how these changes have impacted all aspects of the environment and the life it supports. Finally, we will look to the future and imagine the same environment in 100 year's time.

BELOW
Average annual temperature at Vernadsky Station, Argentine Islands.

The changing climate

The first permanently occupied stations on the Antarctic Peninsula were established during the Second World War. From the outset, measuring temperature, pressure, humidity, wind-speed and direction, and cloud cover, was an unbreakable daily ritual at many of these stations. The commitment of so many professional meteorologists, and the cooks, doctors and mechanics that assisted them in collecting these data has left a rich resource for today's climate scientists.

Perhaps the most notable record was collected by hundreds of British, then Ukrainian researchers at Faraday Station in the Argentine Islands, which became Vernadsky Station in 1996. The temperature sequence shows a 3°C (5.4°F) warming over the second half of the twentieth

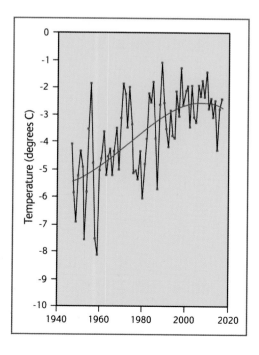

century. The warming appears to plateau around year 2000, and temperatures today remain very high compared to earlier decades.

Similar patterns and rates of warming have been seen elsewhere on the Antarctic Peninsula and its islands, but the question remains whether this is an expression of human-induced climate change, or the result of a locally-variable climate. Ice-core data from James Ross Island do indicate periods of similar warming in the last 2,000 years, and show the rate of warming over last 50 years was unusual, but not unprecedented.

Whatever the underlying cause, it is undoubted that the temperatures experienced on the Antarctic Peninsula in recent decades by plants, animals, and above all the ice, have been higher

ICE CORES – A STORY OF THE PLANET

The long cores of ice that scientists collect from ice sheets contain layers of ice that are progressively older the deeper we go into the ice sheet. This ice contains a record of past temperatures on the planet, and in the bubbles of air captured in the ice provides a record of the composition of our atmosphere. The fact that these two signals are recorded side-by-side, make ice cores the most important single source of data concerning past climate on our planet.

The 3 km (1¾ miles) long ice core from Dome-C in East Antarctica gave us an unbroken record from the present back to 800,000 years ago. Throughout this period, temperature was aligned to the concentrations of the greenhouse gases carbon dioxide and methane, unassailable evidence that it is greenhouse gas concentrations that control the temperature of the planet. During these 800,000 years, natural fluctuations in carbon dioxide were from 180 parts per million (ppm, during full glacial conditions) to 260 ppm (during the warm interglacials). The last monitoring station on Earth to see year-round levels in carbon dioxide below 400 ppm was Halley VI Research Station, East Antarctica.

Collecting the deepest ice cores, which is done in short segments, is a long and difficult process. It requires months of work by teams of scientists and engineers working in remote locations, under the harshest of conditions. Currently, European researchers are making the first steps, in a programme called 'Oldest Ice', to acquire ice that is at least 1.4 million years old, from the heart of East Antarctica. Here summer temperatures rarely exceed -25°C (-13°F), darkness prevails for months, and altitude sickness is an additional concern.

Finally, it is worth noting one other specifically Antarctic factor. Human activity has led to thinning of the ozone layer in the atmosphere over Antarctica (see p. 45). Interactions between the Ozone Hole high in the stratosphere (at 14 to 20 km altitude or 8¾ to 12½ miles) and the lower atmosphere have increased the strength of the westerly winds that blow round the continent. This may well have been a factor in the Antarctic Peninsula warming, and may well have slowed warming over the rest of the continent. As the ozone hole declines over the coming decades scientists expect this effect to lessen, with warming across the continent accelerating in coming decades.

OPPOSITE Carbon dioxide levels and temperature over time, from Antarctic ice core data.

than the norm in recent centuries, and this has had significant impacts on those systems; and even without additional warming, such changes are likely to continue long into the future.

Changing glaciers

As has been mentioned (see p. 56), glaciers naturally reach equilibrium with climate. But when a change in winter snowfall or summer melting occurs, or there is a change in the temperature of the ocean into which they flow, glaciers must readjust their size and shape to find a new equilibrium. In recent decades, glaciers along the west coast of the Antarctic Peninsula have retreated in their hundreds. One recent

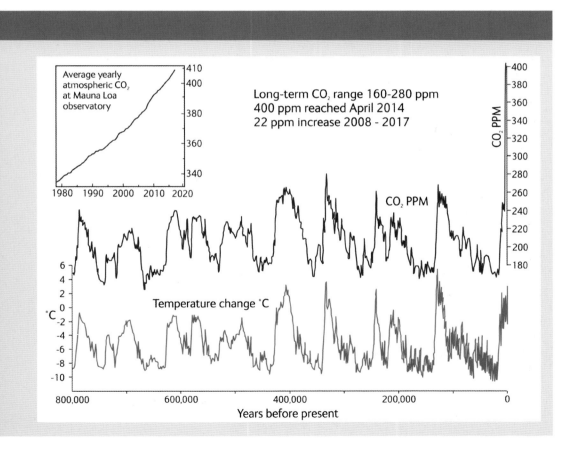

Average yearly atmospheric CO_2 at Mauna Loa observatory

Long-term CO_2 range 160-280 ppm
400 ppm reached April 2014
22 ppm increase 2008 - 2017

CO_2 PPM

Temperature change °C

Years before present

study showed that 87% of glaciers had retreated, some only by tens of metres, but others by up to several kilometres. Shortening of the glaciers has made them steeper, so that they flow faster into the ocean. Recent research has shown that while the atmospheric warming may have had a role, it is the change in the sea temperatures that has been most influential.

The diversity of behaviour of individual glaciers, however, emphasises the danger of using a single glacier as a representative example, or 'benchmark'. The map opposite shows how glaciers are fiercely individual, with changes in two neighbouring glaciers being quite different. Although both glaciers have retreated several kilometres since the 1950s, the Widdowson Glacier retreated substantially between 1997 and 2001, while its near neighbour Drummond Glacier barely showed a change. It is likely that the large retreat of Widdowson Glacier occurred because of its particular geometry. Prior to 1997 the flow was being forced to converge by the shape of the bay in which it was contained. After a small retreat into the bay had occurred, the stabilising effect of this convergence was lost, and 5 km (3 miles) of rapid retreat occurred before it found another stable configuration. So, while the origin of retreat lies in the changing environment, the response of individual glaciers is more nuanced.

RIGHT
Glacier retreat on the Antarctic Peninsula.

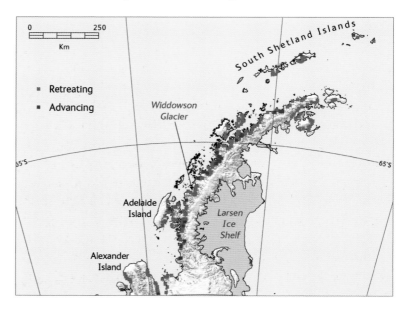

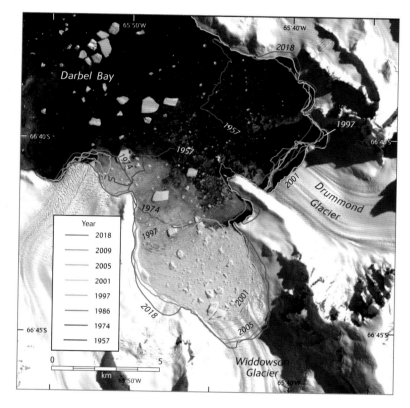

LEFT
Widdowson and Drummond glaciers – an example of glacier retreat on the Antarctic Peninsula. Note the flotilla of icebergs that have broken away from the glacier front and are drifting into Darbel Bay. Image date 2001.

Ice shelves

Ice shelves occur where a glacier manages to flow off the land, and begins to float without either melting or breaking up into icebergs. They surround most of the Antarctic coastline apart from the north-west Antarctic Peninsula (see p. 59).

In recent years, scientists have understood the reason that ice shelves are not present here in terms of a 'climatic limit of viability' for ice shelves. This limit is roughly coincident with the -9 °C (16 °F) mean (average) annual air temperature, but is more correctly viewed as the limit at which significant summer melting occurs on the surface of the ice (p. 98). South of this limit, ice shelves are present around much of the Antarctic coast, but north of it, they do not survive. In recent decades, as climate has warmed, the limit has moved south with dramatic effects on the coastline of the Antarctic Peninsula.

At least nine ice shelves on the Antarctic Peninsula have shown signs of retreat linked to climate change in recent decades. This is different from the normal processes of cyclical advance and retreat associated with iceberg formation. Wordie Ice Shelf was the first, in the early 1990s, and for the first time satellite images allowed scientists to map its progressive retreat in detail. This was followed, in 1995, by the rapid collapse of several ice shelves on the east coast of the peninsula, after several decades of retreat. These included

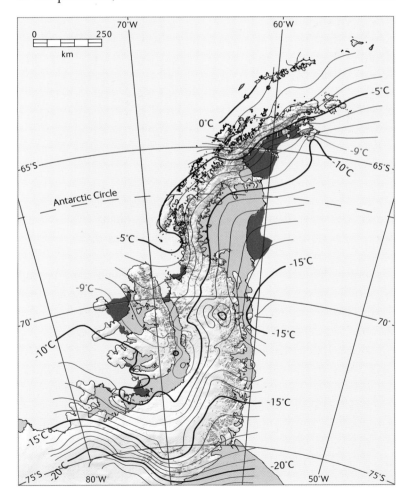

RIGHT
Mean annual temperatures and ice-shelf retreat.

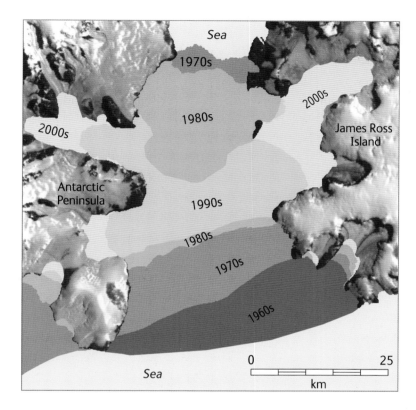

Sea

1970s

2000s

1980s

2000s

James Ross Island

Antarctic Peninsula

1990s

1980s

1970s

1960s

0   25

Sea

km

LEFT
Retreat of the Prince Gustav
Ice Shelf.

Larsen Ice Shelf A which collapsed into an armada of ship-sized icebergs that floated out into the Weddell Sea where they eventually melted.

Around the same time the Prince Gustav Ice Shelf broke up and opened the passage between James Ross Island and the mainland for the first time in recorded history. Early in 1997, the Greenpeace ship, *MV Arctic Sunrise*, became the first to successfully navigate the channel and circumnavigate James Ross Island.

In 2002, the collapse of Larsen Ice Shelf B made global headlines. The event had been predicted by British Antarctic Survey scientists who had previously studied the Wordie, Prince Gustav and Larsen A ice shelves, but they had not expected it to occur so soon. There was widespread astonishment when satellite images revealed that in just 40 days more than 3,200 km^2 (1,235 miles^2) of ice shattered into small icebergs and floated out to sea.

Since 2002, several other ice shelves along both coasts of the Antarctic Peninsula have retreated, most recently Wilkins Ice Shelf in 2009. Many glaciologists believe that Larsen Ice Shelf C will be the next to retreat. A significant iceberg, called A68, calved away from Larsen C, but only time will tell if this is the beginning of retreat or just another iceberg (see p. 60).

ABOVE
The Larsen A Ice Shelf breaking up into thousands of icebergs in January 1995. Around 1,300 km² (502 miles²) of ice shelf were lost in 50 days. This photograph is looking west over the Larsen A towards Drygalski Glacier, with the high plateau of Graham Land on the horizon and part of Seal Nunataks just visible to the south.

The pattern and sequence of the retreat of ice shelves around the Antarctic Peninsula has produced two important insights for glaciologists. The first was the identification of the climatic 'limit of viability', the second is an answer to the question, 'how much does the presence of an ice shelf act to stabilise the (grounded) glaciers that feed it?' The answer has come from an analysis of the glaciers that fed Larsen A and B. In each case, the loss of those ice shelves caused a dramatic increase in ice-flow on the glaciers that fed them. Drygalski Glacier, for example, started to accelerate soon after the collapse of Larsen A, in 1995, by 1999 it had more than doubled its speed, and this speed was maintained at least until 2007, when the last measurement was reported. The future of the much larger ice shelves further south, and the massive ice sheets that they protect, may become clearer through research into current changes on the Antarctic Peninsula.

Sea ice

Sea ice is probably one of the most complex and difficult to understand features of the Antarctic environment. It feels the influence of water temperature which causes it to freeze then to melt, winds and ocean currents that move it from place-to-place, and snowfall which makes it thicker. It is this complexity that has led Antarctic sea ice to change over recent decades in an apparently perverse way.

Daily satellite observations of sea-ice extent are now available for Antarctica for more than 30 years, long enough that climatologists accept them as 'long-term' records. These records show an extraordinary pattern of change. Around the west of the Antarctic Peninsula the effect is apparently consistent with recent atmospheric warming. Here we see up to 100 days fewer of sea-ice cover each year, but elsewhere around Antarctica, the change is the opposite with increasing days of sea-ice cover. The answer may simply be in the winds that drive sea ice away from the Antarctic continent, and stronger winds drive the sea ice further offshore so that it covers a greater area. So while the area covered by sea ice is increasing, it is perhaps, on average thinner. Newly-developed techniques to measure sea-ice thickness using satellites will, in time, likely confirm this hypothesis.

Impact on life on land

The impact of climate warming on terrestrial plants and animals is not simply the result of warming of the ground on which they lie. For plants, the dominant factor is often the increase in the availability of water as snow and ice melts more frequently, together with the area of snow-free ground available for colonization. Both factors lengthen the period of plant growth and, in future, both factors may reduce environmental stress, promoting growth, and increasing population numbers and biomass. However, with this may also come increased competition and displacement of slow-growing organisms.

Until recently, only two examples of vegetation response to increasing temperatures on the Antarctic Peninsula were reported. Both of the vascular, or higher, plants that live on the Antarctic Peninsula, *Deschampsia antarctica* and *Colobanthus quitensis* increased in number between 1960s and 2010, and both have shown a southward migration. More recently, other plants such as lichens and mosses have shown similar responses, and it is clear that the ecology of the Antarctic Peninsula is changing rapidly.

Similarly, the animals that call the peninsula home, or at least, make it a frequent port of call, have also changed their behaviour. Their responses are largely due to changes in food availability and their access to it, but the fundamental cause is changing climate.

In several cases that access to food rests on sea ice conditions. For example; some penguins need sea ice to provide them access to the seas, and others do not. The so-called, *ice-obligate* species (e.g., emperor and Adélie) have shifted south and their nesting range contracted as sea ice has become less abundant. Meanwhile, the *ice-intolerant* species (e.g., gentoo and chinstrap) have expanded their range southward and occupy more nesting sites (see map pp. 138–139).

The future

Most projections of Antarctic climate suggest that warming will continue, and perhaps intensify, during the twenty-first century. They do not, however, agree on how much warming will occur or whether it will be concentrated in the summer or winter. Nonetheless, it is a reasonable question for everyone visiting the Antarctica Peninsula to ask, how long will this unique landscape with its fascinating flora and fauna survive in a form that would be recognizable today?

For the glaciers and ice shelves, changes have already been profound, and in future we expect to see other ice shelves and glaciers retreat. Where once the glaciers flowed directly into the sea, they will retreat into the fjords and eventually onto the land. Some will become 'land-terminating glaciers', similar to those we see in sub-Antarctic islands, Patagonia and in mountain ranges around the world. Indeed, in a hundred years, it is possible that northern parts of the Antarctic Peninsula may come to resemble southern Greenland, or even the coast of Alaska, with glacier snouts ending on coastal flats and meltwater streams taking their water to the sea. Such a retreat would contribute to global sea-level rise, but that contribution would be small compared to the likely contribution from the huge glaciers of West Antarctica. However, the local significance of such change should not be under-estimated; this new landscape would have a great deal more exposed rock, and provide colonization and migration opportunities for plants and animals.

The potential impact of future warming on flora and fauna is similarly grave, especially where it is compounded by growing other, non-climatic, stresses. One alarming example of this is the potential interaction of climate change and increasing visitor numbers on the Antarctic Peninsula. The warming of the Antarctic Peninsula climate will undoubtedly reduce the climatic barriers by which the currently cold and dry conditions protect the peninsula environment from colonization by non-native species. Within decades, species that previously only thrived on warmer sub-Antarctic islands, may for the first time be able to survive on the Antarctic Peninsula. Plants, insects and even pests, such as mice and rats, may gain sufficient hold to establish themselves, and retreating glaciers could allow routes for dispersal. In a further jeopardy, the barriers to colonization may be reduced at the same time that opportunities for invasive species to travel aboard ships and aircraft to the Antarctic Peninsula are increasing. Indeed, recent increases in tourism, and in scientific activity, have already multiplied the possibility of transfer of soil, seeds and even live plants and animals enormously in recent years.

Recognizing this combined threat has led most organizations responsible for travel to Antarctica to establish strong biosecurity protocols to reduce this opportunity. Nevertheless, it is the responsibility of all visitors, whether we are tourists or scientists to ensure we do everything in our power to prevent those alien invaders from reaching this special corner of Antarctica.

JOHN SHEARS AND STUART DOUBLEDAY
THE ANTARCTIC TREATY

THE ANTARCTIC TREATY OF 1959 and its related agreements govern all activities in Antarctica. This system of international governance is unique and of global importance. It established the continent as a region of peace and science, and set territorial claims to one side. It is considered to be one of the most successful international treaties ever made.

Of the many countries that have taken part in the exploration of Antarctica, only seven have staked territorial claims in the region. They are Argentina, Australia, Chile, France, New Zealand, Norway and the UK. The UK was the first to claim territory in Antarctica, in 1908. The claims of the UK, Argentina and Chile to the Antarctic Peninsula all overlap and during the 1940s and 1950s the competing claims caused international tension. At the same time, there was also disagreement between the Cold War superpowers of the USA and the USSR about the future use of the continent.

The foundations of the Antarctic Treaty were laid during the International Geophysical Year (IGY) in 1957–58. Twelve countries all agreed to take part (Argentina, Australia, Belgium, Chile, France, Japan, New Zealand, Norway, South Africa, UK, USA and the USSR) and join together to undertake scientific research in Antarctica. The IGY was a tremendous success and resulted in significant scientific research and discoveries, and the setting up of several Antarctic research stations still operating today. Perhaps the greatest legacy of the IGY is that it eased political tensions and encouraged the participating countries to look for a permanent international solution to manage Antarctica. This led directly to the agreement of the Antarctic Treaty.

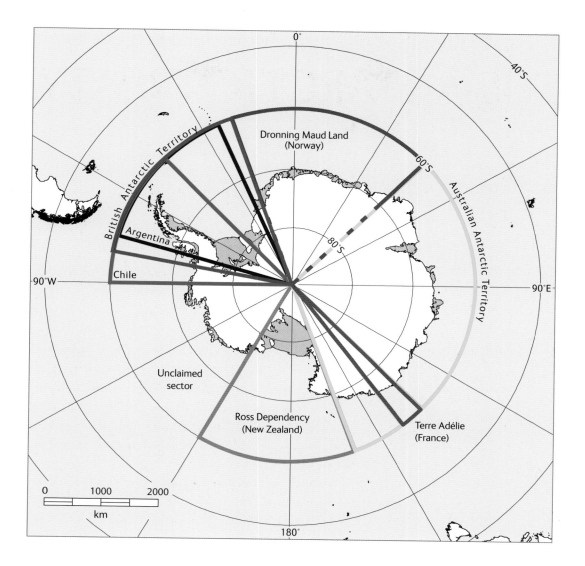

After 18 months of negotiations, the Antarctic Treaty was signed on 1 December 1959 in Washington, USA, by the 12 nations that had participated in the IGY. The UK was the first country to ratify the Treaty, which entered into force on 23 June 1961. It was a historic and important agreement and began a new era in Antarctic history. The objectives of the Antarctic Treaty are simple but unique in international relations. In summary, the Treaty sets out the following.

ABOVE
Seven nations have made territorial claims in Antarctica, but these are put to one side under the Antarctic Treaty.

- Sets aside disputes over territorial sovereignty.
- Prohibits military activities, such as the establishment of military bases or weapons testing and prohibits nuclear explosions and the disposal of radioactive waste.
- Guarantees freedom of scientific research and promotes international scientific cooperation with scientific results exchanged and made freely available.
- Provides for the inspection of all stations, ships and equipment in Antarctica to ensure compliance with the Treaty.
- Covers the area south of 60° South latitude.

The Treaty remains in force indefinitely and its success is shown by the steady growth in membership. In 2018, a total of 53 countries, comprising over 80% of the world's population, are signatories. Consultative (voting) status is held by 29 countries who have demonstrated their commitment to the Antarctic by conducting significant scientific research in the region. The Treaty nations meet every year to discuss a wide range of issues relating to governing and protecting the continent. All decisions are agreed by consensus.

Under the umbrella of the Treaty, further conventions and protocols have been developed to address issues of Antarctic natural resource management and protection of the environment. The

BELOW
An expedition tour ship at Jenny Island, Marguerite Bay. The Antarctic Peninsula is receiving an increasing number of tour-ship visitors.

original Treaty did not address such issues as they were not considered priorities in the late 1950s! The most important additions are the Protocol on Environmental Protection and the Convention on the Conservation of Antarctic Marine Living Resources (CCAMLR). Each of these agreements was, in its time, acknowledged as a trailblazer in international environmental law.

The Protocol on Environmental Protection

Antarctica remains the last great wilderness on Earth. In the past, the continent was protected by its remoteness and inaccessibility, but due to modern technology this is no longer the case and Antarctica is receiving an increasing number of visitors. International concern over the conservation of the continent in the late 1980s led to the Treaty nations developing the Protocol on Environmental Protection to the Antarctic Treaty, which came into force in 1998. It provides for the comprehensive protection of the Antarctic environment and sets out mandatory regulations governing human activities in the region. As a result Antarctica is protected by one of the toughest sets of environmental regulations found anywhere in the world. The Environmental Protocol commits the Treaty nations to the

'comprehensive protection of the Antarctic environment' by setting out the following.

- Setting out principles for environmental protection.
- Banning all mineral resource activity (other than scientific research).
- Requiring an Environmental Impact Assessment (EIA) for all activities before they are allowed to go ahead.
- Encouraging cooperation and exchange of information between the Treaty nations about environmental issues in Antarctica.

The Treaty nations have implemented the Environmental Protocol in their own national legislation. For example, in the UK the Protocol is implemented through the two Antarctic Acts (1994 and 2013). Whilst the Environmental Protocol protects all of the Antarctic Treaty area as a 'natural reserve devoted to peace and science', certain parts of the continent are so important they are given even greater protection through a system of specially protected and managed areas and historic sites.

Antarctic Specially Protected Areas

An area of Antarctica may be designated an Antarctic Specially Protected Area (ASPA) to protect outstanding environmental, scientific, historic, aesthetic or wilderness values. Entry to ASPAs is prohibited except with a permit. Activities within ASPAs must comply with a management plan, and access is usually only allowed for scientific research or monitoring. There are over 70 ASPAs around the continent, many of which are located on the Antarctic Peninsula. ASPAs protect populations of penguins and other birds (Ardley Island, Avian Island), important geological features (fumaroles on Deception Island), areas with exceptionally well-developed vegetation (Moe Island, Lynch Island, Green Island) or acting as control sites to monitor the environmental impacts of research stations (Rothera Point).

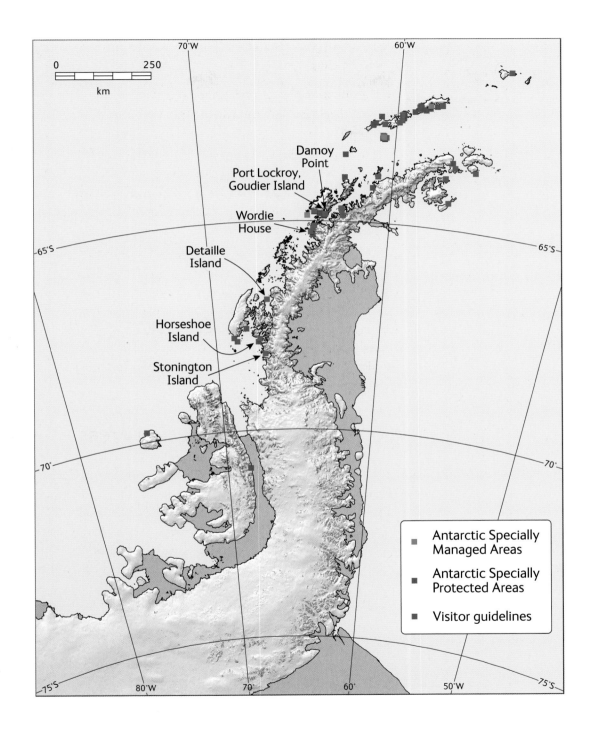

Antarctic Specially Managed Areas (ASMAs) are areas where human activities need to be coordinated to avoid possible conflicts, improve scientific cooperation or minimise environmental impacts. For example, an area around a research station, or where two or more stations are close by, could be designated an ASMA. Entry to ASMAs does not require a permit, but activities within ASMAs are coordinated by a management plan. There are six ASMAs in Antarctica, of which three are located on the Antarctic Peninsula (see map on p. 109), including Admiralty Bay, King George Island and Deception Island. Although ASMAs and ASPAs can be designated under the Environmental Protocol to protect special marine areas, there are currently only six entirely marine ASPAs. Marine protected areas can also be designated under CCAMLR. In 2010, CCAMLR created the first 'high seas' Marine Protected Area (MPA) south of the South Orkney Islands, based on a proposal from the UK. In this area of about 94,000 km² (about 37,000 square miles), which is larger than Portugal or Minnesota, USA, all fishing activities are banned.

BELOW
Moss bank at Coppermine Peninsula ASPA 112, Robert Island. South Shetland Islands.

Historic sites in Antarctica

Sites of historic importance can be protected as Historic Sites and Monuments (HSMs). There are over 90 HSMs in Antarctica, with

many found on the Antarctic Peninsula. They are mostly bases, huts and other features associated with early exploration of the continent, or graves and memorials to people who have died in Antarctica. One of the most well known historic sites on the Antarctic Peninsula is the UK 'Base A' at Port Lockroy (HSM No. 61), on Goudier Island, off Wiencke Island.

Visitor guidelines

Despite the success of the Environmental Protocol, concerns have remained about environmental impact at frequently visited sites. In 2005, the Treaty nations adopted the concept of guidelines for popular visitor sites. In 2018 there were guidelines for 42 sites around Antarctica (see map p. 109). All the most popular visitor sites on the Antarctic Peninsula, such as Port Lockroy, Neko Harbour, Cuverville Island and Half Moon Island, now have specific visitor guidelines. The aim of the guidelines is to provide practical guidance and information for visitors on how they should undertake visits to the sites, taking into account their wildlife and historical importance, any scientific equipment and potential hazards.

THE UK ANTARCTIC HERITAGE TRUST

The United Kingdom Antarctic Heritage Trust (UKAHT) works to conserve historic buildings and artefacts in Antarctica, ensuring the legacy of past endeavour in Antarctica is secured for future generations. The Trust manages six British bases on the Antarctic Peninsula that have been designated HSMs supported by an active public engagement programme. It works closely with the British Government, British Antarctic Survey, and the International Association of Antarctica Tour Operators (IAATO).

These six sites represent different periods in British involvement and science on the Antarctic Peninsula and are accessible to visitors. Port Lockroy has been restored to its 1950s condition, but the others are conserved as they were found, making them unique time capsules of human endeavour in this extreme environment.

UKAHT SITES

UKAHT manages a long term conservation programme to care for the six historic sites so that they might be enjoyed and understood by future generations.

Each of the six historic sites (see map on p. 109) has its own fascinating story, but together they tell the story of British scientific endeavour in Antarctica since the Second World War.

PORT LOCKROY (BASE A), HSM 61

Port Lockroy is a sheltered harbour off the coast of Wiencke Island and offers some of the most dramatic mountain and glacier scenery on the Antarctic Peninsula. For more than a century Port Lockroy has been a home for explorers, whalers, sailors and scientists and it has since become one of the most popular visitor sites in Antarctica today.

It is of significant historical importance because it was established by the Royal Navy in 1944 during World War II as part of 'Operation Tabarin'. This was a military operation to deter enemy use of sheltered harbours on the Antarctic Peninsula and to provide meteorological reports for allied shipping. After the war, Port Lockroy was handed over to the predecessor of the British Antarctic Survey, which ran a programme of important scientific research at the base examining the physics of the upper atmosphere. Base A was a key monitoring site during the IGY in 1957–58. Following its closure in January 1962, the wooden buildings gradually fell into disrepair. After a conservation survey in 1994 by the UK Antarctic Heritage Trust, and designation as an HSM, the buildings were renovated and restored by the British Antarctic Survey in 1996 and their care passed to UKAHT in 2006. The site is now maintained as a living museum with curated displays in room settings which tell the story of the base in its heyday in the late 1950s. There are artefacts and ephemera which interpret the life and work of the base. Alongside the museum is an operational post office and gift shop, which support the work of the Trust. Around Port Lockroy there are artefacts from the whaling era, when it was used as a safe and sheltered harbour, plus a colony of gentoo penguins.

ABOVE Port Lockroy with a glimpse of the spectacular Fief Mountains behind.

WORDIE HOUSE (BASE F), HSM 62

Wordie House was established on 7 January 1947, on Winter Island, Argentine Islands. The hut is named after James Wordie, the chief scientist and geologist on Shackleton's *Endurance* expedition 1914–17. The hut stands on the foundations of an earlier building, used by the British Graham Land Expedition from 1935–36.

The most important scientific research carried out at Wordie House was in meteorology and the work here began one of the longest and most important meteorological recording programmes in the Antarctic. Recording instruments were housed in meteorological screens, one of which can still be seen today a short distance to the east of the hut, and balloons were released daily to gather meteorological data.

Wordie House was designated an HSM in 1995 and has been in the care of UKAHT since 2009. Initial conservation works and making the hut weather-tight have been completed, and there are around 500 original artefacts on site.

ABOVE Wordie House, Winter Island, Argentine Islands.

HORSESHOE ISLAND (BASE Y) HSM 63

Horseshoe was established as a scientific base in March 1955 and closed in August 1960. Research carried out here included geology, meteorology and topographic survey. Extensive survey trips covering hundreds of miles and lasting several months were often undertaken from the station using dog teams and sledges. The site consists of the original main building, a weather balloon shed, dog pens and emergency store. Inside, the station contains almost all of its original contents, fixtures and fittings, including kitchen utensils, stocks of food and fuel, workshop tools, radio equipment, and a diesel generator. Horseshoe was designated HSM No. 63 in 1995 and has been managed by UKAHT since 2014 and was the focus of the UKAHT conservation programme in 2016–17. The excellent condition and completeness of both the buildings and artefacts are of considerable historical significance; together they provide a very special time-capsule of British life and science in the Antarctic during the late 1950s.

ABOVE. Base Y, Horseshoe Island, Marguerite Bay.

STONINGTON ISLAND (BASE E) HSM NO. 64

Stonington, in Marguerite Bay, operated from 1946–50 and then again from 1960–75 after which the base permanently closed. This building is the second British hut built on the island and was originally used as a base for sledging operations in the area. During this time, epic and historic journeys lasting several months and covering hundreds of miles were made using dog sledges. As a result, much of the mapping of the Antarctic Peninsula was completed by the men operating from here. The base closed in 1950 due to continuing difficulties in relief by ship, caused by bad sea ice conditions.

Stonington Island is also the location of the US East Base. The neighbouring American base was established in 1939 by the US Antarctic Service Expedition and then later reoccupied in 1947–48 by the Ronne Antarctic Research Expedition. This marked a period of cooperation between the two stations and between the UK and USA.

In 1960, after 10 years, the British base reopened and a new hut was erected (still standing) as the centre for fieldwork in the southern Antarctic Peninsula. The research in these later years focused on geology, glaciology and meteorology and continued until the station finally closed in February 1975.

UKAHT SITES

The British hut currently standing at Stonington, is a steel-framed hut and the first two-storey building to be erected by the British Antarctic Survey. It marked the beginning of modern construction techniques. As well as the main building the station also comprises of a number of other structures: the generator shed, pup pens, emergency store, radio mast, water tank and the collapsed anemometer tower. The base has been managed by UKAHT since 2014, including a major maintenance campaign in 2017–18. The buildings are in relatively good condition, but only a few of the original artefacts remain on site.

ABOVE Base W, Detaille Island.

ABOVE Base E, Stonington Island, Marguerite Bay.

DETAILLE ISLAND (STATION W) HSM 83

The station was established on Detaille Island, in Crystal Sound, in February 1956 as a base for topographic survey, geology and meteorology. It was evacuated and closed in March 1959 when sea ice and weather made relief by ship impossible and operations were transferred to Horseshoe Island (Station Y). Detaille operated for just three short years and in spite of the difficulties, much was achieved in terms of geological mapping and surveying of the surrounding areas.

The site was cleaned up and maintained periodically by BAS during the 1990s. It was designated as Historic Site No. 83 under the Antarctic Treaty in 2009 and has been managed by UKAHT since October 2009. Since the base's closure it has remained unoccupied and relatively unaltered. The ice conditions still make it difficult to reach Detaille, however, sea ice permitting, tourist vessels occasionally manage to visit the site.

DAMOY HUT, HSM NO. 84

Damoy Hut which stands in Dorian Bay on Wiencke Island, close to Damoy Point, is the most modern of Britain's Historic Sites and Monuments in Antarctica. The hut was perfectly located to serve as a British summer air facility and transit station for scientists travelling further south. The bay gave good access for ship launch craft and the glacier on Wiencke Island was found to be a suitable skiway for aircraft. Damoy was closed in 2004–05 when it was superseded by an airstrip at Rothera Research Station which enabled direct flights from the Falkland Islands. The hut is well preserved and still holds original objects and equipment offering a glimpse of life on base.

ABOVE Refuge hut at Damoy, Wiencke Island.

The Convention on the Conservation of Antarctic Marine Living Resources

The Convention on the Conservation of Antarctic Marine Living Resources (CCAMLR) came into force in 1982 to protect the marine ecosystem in the Southern Ocean and regulate fisheries.

It was established in response to concerns by the Treaty nations in the late 1970s that increasing catches of krill, the small shrimp-like animals that are an important part of the Southern Ocean foodchain, could have a serious effect on the marine ecosystem.

The aim of the Convention is to conserve marine life in the Southern Ocean. It does not ban fishing or harvesting, as long as they are carried out in a sustainable way. The Convention established an International Commission to manage marine living resources in the Southern Ocean, based on scientific understanding of its ecosystem. In 2018, a total of 24 countries, and the European Union, are voting members of the Commission, and a further 11 nations have signed the Convention.

The boundary of CCAMLR is not the same as the Antarctic Treaty Area. CCAMLR extends further north and is delimited by the Antarctic Convergence (also called the Polar Front), which is formed where the cold Antarctic waters meet the warmer waters of more temperate zones. The Antarctic Convergence acts as an effective biological barrier, and the Southern Ocean is effectively a closed ecosystem.

LEFT
The Antarctic krill, *Euphausia superba*, is a key species in the Antarctic foodchain. Krill grow to about 6 cm (2.4 in) long, often occurring in dense swarms.

ADRIAN FOX

PLACE NAMES

ONE OF THE BEST WAYS to understand the complex geography of the Antarctic Peninsula is to follow a ship's track on a good map. When tracing a route through the straits and channels between offshore islands, and past the headlands, bays, mountains and glaciers of the mainland, the keen map-reader will notice the great variety of place names and be curious about their origins.

Place names are important for accurately and precisely referring to a place. In regions that have a long history of human occupation every place and every feature that needs a name has a name, but the Antarctic Peninsula was first visited less than 200 years ago. There has never been a native population and explorers and cartographers were presented with a blank canvas. So place names here are a kind of shorthand for the history of exploration over the last two centuries and are often a fascinating glimpse of the hardships and adventures of the explorers and scientists who were the first to visit these uncharted lands.

Throughout history place names, together with mapping, have been a way of projecting political authority and power in a region. This is very true in Antarctica where place names have long been seen as a way to 'fly the flag' and leave a lasting record of national interests in an area. As a result, many of the names for the most prominent features, especially those visible from the sea, trace the early exploration by national expeditions. Over the late nineteenth and early twentieth centuries, successive expeditions slowly put together the complex jigsaw puzzle of the intricate geography of the Antarctic Peninsula and this piece-by-piece progress is reflected in the clusters of related place names that appear on maps today.

OPPOSITE
Progress of exploration and principal sources of place names.

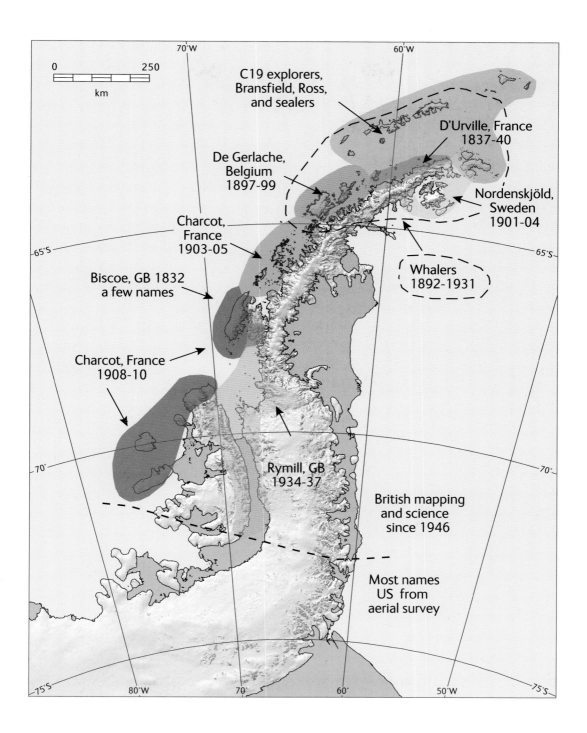

C19 explorers,
Bransfield, Ross,
and sealers

D'Urville, France
1837-40

De Gerlache,
Belgium
1897-99

Nordenskjöld,
Sweden
1901-04

Charcot,
France
1903-05

Whalers
1892-1931

Biscoe, GB 1832
a few names

Charcot, France
1908-10

Rymill, GB
1934-37

British mapping
and science
since 1946

Most names
US from
aerial survey

Early exploration and the first place names

The South Shetland Islands were the first part of the Antarctic Peninsula region to be discovered when Captain William Smith in the Royal Navy ship *Williams* sighted, roughly charted and named Williams Point on Livingston Island on 19 February 1819. Smith returned later in 1819 as navigator on an expedition captained by Edward Bransfield, again in the *Williams*. Although hampered by sea ice and persistent fog, they sailed west to east along the north coast of the island chain, charting and naming as they went. They then turned along the south coast, landed at King George Bay to claim the island for Great Britain, and reached Deception Island, glimpsed through fog in January 1820. They then struck south to discover Trinity Island and make the first sighting of the mainland on 30 January 1820. A further west to east journey took them along the north coast of Trinity Peninsula as far as Bransfield Island where sea ice forced the *Williams* north to the Elephant Island group.

During this voyage they named 21 of the major islands and topographic features, including King George Island (after King George III), Smith Island (William Smith), Trinity Island, Cornwallis Island, Clarence Island, Cape Bowles and Cape Shirreff (Navy Board and admirals) as well as Tower Island and Desolation Island (descriptive). These first categories of place names – sponsors and figures of national importance; members of the expedition or senior naval officers; and descriptive features – have been broadly followed for place naming in the Antarctic region ever since. With naval reserve, Bransfield didn't name any discoveries after himself. The names Bransfield Strait, Bransfield Island and Mount Bransfield were all applied in the following decades by explorers building on Bransfield's discoveries.

The age of the sealers

Captain James Cook's discovery of South Georgia in 1775, and the huge numbers of seals there, led directly to a sealing industry on the island. Fur seals were slaughtered for their skins and elephant seals for their blubber (oil). Following reckless over-exploitation, fur seals were almost extinct on South Georgia by 1820 and when Smith's report of new land further south became known, it was inevitable that sealers would push south to the Antarctic Peninsula in search of new stocks.

A number of sealing expeditions took place between 1820 and 1825 that gradually sketched in the geography of the South Shetland Islands and the northern tip of the Antarctic Peninsula. The sealers didn't always report their findings, preferring to keep their discoveries to themselves to protect the lucrative trade. Furthermore, as they were operating simultaneously but independently, they often saw the same new features at about the same time, so it has proved difficult to establish a reliable chronology of discovery. However, the most important sealing expeditions with regard to charting and place names were led by the British captains George Powell, (1820–21 and 1821–22), James Weddell (1821–22), and the American Benjamin Pendleton (1820–21 and 1821–22).

Weddell and Powell both carried out extensive charting along the South Shetland Islands chain. The austral summer of 1820–21 had seen an immense slaughter of fur seals in the South Shetland Islands and in the next summer seals were hard to find, and so both Weddell and Powell pushed further east into the Southern Ocean looking for new sealing grounds and both independently discovered the South Orkney Islands. Weddell was an ex-Royal Navy captain and kept detailed records. He used 54 names in the South Shetland Islands and another 13 in the South Orkney Islands. The South Orkney Islands are named collectively with the South Shetland Islands to reflect their lower latitude, as in the northern hemisphere. Powell compiled a chart of both island groups with 93 names, based on his own investigations and gleanings from other sealers. Powell was able to publish his chart before Weddell's material was available, and so in modern usage his names have had priority over Weddell's in nearly all cases.

Pendleton's expedition comprised five ships. The smallest, the *Hero,* was captained by Nathaniel Palmer who was despatched by Pendleton to search for new sealing grounds. He headed south from the South Shetland Islands and investigated Deception Island, first seen (but not named) by Bransfield in early 1820. Palmer named it in recognition of the deceptive nature of this ring-shaped island with its narrow entrance leading to a superb natural harbour. The *Hero* then sailed south across Bransfield Strait and on 17 November 1820 explored the section of the Antarctic Peninsula between Charcot Bay and the entrance to Orléans Strait. This was later named Palmer Land by Powell on his chart of 1822, but is now believed to be the same stretch of coast seen through fog by Bransfield in January 1820 and named Trinity Land. These names are the origins of the modern Palmer Land and Trinity Peninsula.

Several names in the South Shetland Islands came from the sealers or were applied later to remember the activities of the sealers in the area. There are bays named after sealing ships such as Hero Bay, Harmony Cove, Venus Bay and Emerald Cove; while other locations refer to the home ports of British and American sealers, including Yankee Harbour, Blythe Bay (Blyth, England), Dunbar Islands and Greenwich Island (Connecticut, USA). Neck-or-nothing Passage is a perilous channel west of Blythe Bay used by sealers in desperation to escape gales from the east. Half Moon Island is a succinct description of this natural harbour.

BELOW
The sheltered natural harbour of Half Moon Island, South Shetland Islands.

The age of nationalist exploration

By the austral summer of 1824–25 the fur-seal populations of the South Shetland Islands, South Orkneys and Antarctic Peninsula were almost wiped out by over hunting. Once the sealing industry became unviable, the pace of exploration slowed in the following decades. Nevertheless, most of the major coastal geographic features and prominent inland landmarks visible from the sea were first named during a period of successive national expeditions. These started in the 1830s, and gradually extended south understanding of the complex geography of the Antarctic Peninsula. These expeditions mixed geographical exploration and scientific objectives, such as meteorological measurements, with more nationalistic goals. Not surprisingly, many of the place names from these expeditions refer to politicians, prominent national figures and expedition sponsors, as well as expedition members and descriptive names. This chapter does not attempt a comprehensive survey of expeditions in this period, but summarises those that have left a substantial and enduring legacy of place names on the northern Antarctic Peninsula.

HENRY FOSTER, ROYAL NAVY, 1828–31

Foster landed on what he thought was the mainland to claim it for Great Britain, but was actually Hoseason Island (Possession Point, Chanticleer Point – Foster's ship, named later), and made a detailed survey at Deception Island (Port Foster) including gravity and astronomical observations (Pendulum Cove, Mt Pond – a leading astronomer).

JOHN BISCOE, 1830–33

Biscoe circumnavigated the Southern Ocean and sailed northwards along the west coast of the Antarctic Peninsula, starting at Adelaide Island (Queen Consort of England), where he saw the mountains of Alexander Island to the south and the mainland to the east. Continuing north he discovered and charted the Biscoe Islands, and landed on Anvers Island, which he thought part of the mainland, annexed it for William IV, and named it Graham Land (Sir James

Graham, Head of the Admiralty). He thus extended knowledge of the Antarctic Peninsula south by another four degrees of latitude – about 400 km (250 miles) – to Adelaide Island, with sight of the high mountains of Alexander Island in the distance.

DUMONT D'URVILLE, FRENCH ANTARCTIC EXPEDITION, 1837–40

The main focus of this expedition was the South Pacific, but they also had the aim of achieving a new 'furthest south'. After being denied entrance into the Weddell Sea by ice at the end of February 1838, D'Urville travelled along the north coast of Trinity Peninsula, which he named after the King of France (now preserved as Louis Philippe Plateau) as far south as Orléans Strait. The expedition named 25 of the features along this stretch of coast, mainly after members of the ship's crew (Astrolabe Island – the ship, Cape Ducorps, Montravel Rock, Cape Roquemaurel) and French dignitaries (Joinville Island – Prince of Joinville).

JAMES CLARK ROSS, 1839–43

This British naval expedition explored the area to the east of Trinity Peninsula and left a legacy of 15 names for the major features there, mainly commemorating the navy and senior naval figures: Erebus and Terror Gulf (expedition ships); Admiralty Sound; Seymour Island (naval admiral); Moody Point (Governor of the Falkland Islands). Some locations were named descriptively (Snow Hill Island and Danger Islands).

EDUARD DALLMANN, GERMAN ANTARCTIC EXPEDITION, 1873–74

After visiting the South Orkneys and South Shetland Islands, the expedition steamed down the west side of the Antarctic Peninsula as far south as the Biscoe Islands, but to the west side of Anvers Island and Brabant Island. Their route is marked by 14 names, mostly after prominent figures and patrons of the expedition: Dallmann Bay; Wilhelm Archipelago (Kaiser Wilhelm II); Bismarck Strait (first chancellor of the German Empire); Petermann Island (a leading German cartographer); and Cape Grönland at the northern tip of Anvers Island (after their ship, the first steam ship to reach Antarctica).

ADRIEN DE GERLACHE, BELGIAN ANTARCTIC EXPEDITION, 1897–99

This well-supported expedition made a major contribution to understanding the geography of the northwest coast of Graham Land, by mapping to a new level of detail, reflected in the 45 place names in use today. As usual, these include prominent Belgians and supporters of the expedition – Wilhelmina Bay (Queen of the Netherlands); Lemaire Channel (Belgian explorer); Cape Renard (Belgian Royal Academist); Dannebrog Islands (the Danish flag) – and regions of

BELOW

An extract from a British Antarctic Survey 1:1,000,000 scale map showing names from the de Gerlache expedition in the Anvers Island area (red).

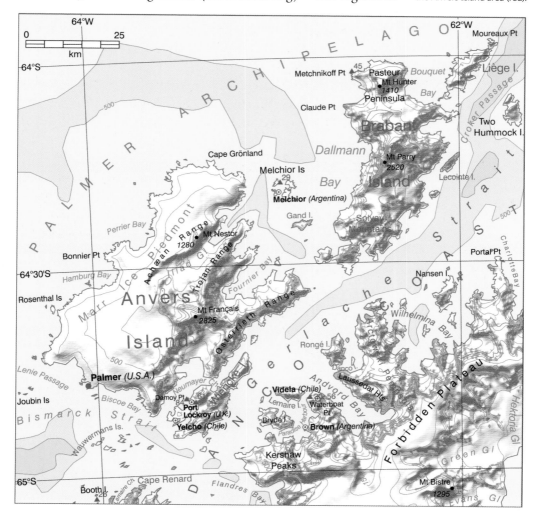

Belgium such as Anvers Island, Brabant Island and Flandres Bay. Additionally, de Gerlache allowed each crew member to propose two names. This means that home towns, family members and crew members occur, leading to an interesting mix of Walloon and Flemish names: Liège Island, Gand Island (Belgian city and town); Félicie Point (girl's name); Wiencke Island (after a sailor who drowned on the expedition). De Gerlache named the whole area Palmer Archipelago, after the pioneering sealer, and was himself honoured with Gerlache Strait. After sighting Alexander Island in February 1898, the ship was beset in ice in the Bellingshausen Sea and drifted for over a year, with great hardship for those on board, who became the first men to overwinter in Antarctica, before finally returning to Chile.

OTTO NORDENSKJÖLD, SWEDISH ANTARCTIC EXPEDITION, 1901–04

This expedition significantly improved knowledge about the north-eastern part of Graham Land. The ship's captain was Carl Larsen, who had previously visited the area on an expedition to search for whales and so already had some first-hand knowledge of the geography. His expedition is included in a discussion of the contributions of the whalers in a later section.

In February 1902 Nordenskjöld made the first passage of Antarctic Sound (expedition ship), and then established a wintering hut on Snow Hill Island (now Antarctic Treaty Historic Site and Monument 38). The ship then returned to the Falkland Islands for the winter. In the southern autumn and spring of 1902, Nordenskjöld pioneered overland dog-sledge travel in Antarctica to explore and map Prince Gustav Channel (Crown Prince of Sweden) and the coast south, to within sight of Jason Peninsula (Sjögren Glacier – a Swedish Geologist, Röhss Bay – expedition suppliers, Drygalski Glacier – a German geographer and polar explorer).

In December 1902, on the way to pick up the winterers on Snow Hill Island, the ship dropped off three men, led by Andersson (Andersson Island) at Hope Bay, with the aim of sledging and mapping an overland route to join the wintering party. However they were unable to complete the journey and had to overwinter 1902–03 at Hope Bay. Shortly afterwards their ship *Antarctic* was beset by ice in Erebus and Terror Gulf and eventually crushed in February 1903. The crew were able to escape to Paulet Island, where they built a stone hut and survived a grim winter (Historic Site and Monument 41). Remarkably, given that they had none of the communication aids of today such as radio, all three parties were finally able to meet up and were later rescued by an Argentinian naval ship in November 1903. The chance meeting of the Andersson Hope Bay group and Nordenskjöld on Vega Island is commemorated in the name Cape Well-met. Whilst this is one of the great stories of Antarctic survival, the expedition also achieved an enormous amount of scientific and mapping work and its contribution lives on in its 65 place names.

JEAN-BAPTISTE CHARCOT, FRENCH ANTARCTIC EXPEDITION, 1903–05 AND 1908–10

Charcot's first expedition in the *Français* (Mount Français – Anvers Island) focused on exploration, scientific observations and detailed mapping of the southern end of the Gerlache Strait, Flandres Bay, Bismarck Strait and down to the northern end of the Grandidier Channel during February 1904. They spent the winter of 1904 at Booth Island, living on the ship but building huts ashore for scientific instruments. The ship was able to break free of the sea ice in December and worked south, roughly charting the Biscoe Islands and establishing the general trend of the coast down to Adelaide Island. Despite being hampered by a troublesome engine and ending the expedition by hitting a rock near Adelaide Island and damaging the ship, they added another significant piece in the puzzle of the west coast of Graham Land.

Charcot's second expedition of 1908–10, this time in the *Pourquoi-Pas?* (the French expression 'and why not?'), extended his previous work south through Crystal Sound, past Adelaide Island and into Marguerite Bay, wintering in 1909 at Petermann Island. Continued work extended as far south as northern Alexander Island before returning home in 1910. Charcot was meticulous about naming new features and avoiding duplication for features already identified by previous expeditions. He named 155 features during the first expedition, of which 129 survive into modern usage, with a further 75 from the second. They dominate the naming of the major features of the west coast of Graham Land from Port Lockroy (French politician and supporter) to Charcot Island (his father). Significant geographical features include, north to south: Mount Matin (sponsoring newspaper); Grandidier Channel (President of Paris Geographical Society); Renaud Island (French hydrographer); Loubet and Fallières coasts (presidents); Marguerite Bay (Charcot's wife); Pourquoi Pas Island (second expedition ship); Rouen Mountains (French city); and many more.

BELOW
An extract from a British Antarctic Survey 1:1,000,000 scale map showing names from Charcot's second expedition, 1908–10 in the Marguerite Bay area.

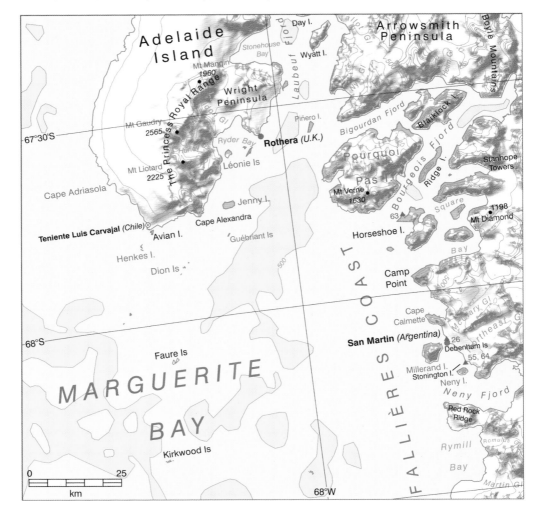

JOHN RYMILL, BRITISH GRAHAM LAND EXPEDITION, 1934–37

This expedition wintered at the Argentine Islands in 1935 and the Debenham Islands in Marguerite Bay in 1936 (see below).

The aim was adventurous exploration to build on Charcot's discoveries, establish whether the Antarctic Peninsula was a continuous feature, and attempt a crossing from west to east. This was to be achieved by a combination of observations from the expedition ship *Penola* (Penola Strait), overland dog-sledging, and aerial reconnaissance in a ski- or float-equipped de Havilland Fox-Moth aircraft. They surveyed the coast and islands of Graham Land from the north end of Brabant Island down to Alexander Island, including sledge journeys through Laubeuf Fjord to the east of Adelaide Island and towards the east coast near the Eternity Range. The expedition's major achievement was to travel down the George VI Sound (King at that time) as far as 72°S.

The expedition named very few places during the survey work, but on his return Rymill made proposals for 103 names based on detailed study of the charts, reports and aerial photographs from the expedition, with a view to using them on new maps and Admiralty charts. This thorough work identified and reconciled numerous problems matching names from previous expeditions with new

LEFT
Penola wintering at Winter Island in the Argentine Islands, 1935.

knowledge about the actual geography. Many of the names are descriptive: Anvil Rock; Dogs Leg Fjord; Ridge Island; The Narrows; and Guardian Rock. Others commemorated supporters of the expedition: Debenham Islands (Director of Scott Polar Research Institute); Goodenough Glacier (wife of the president of the Royal Geographical Society); Batterbee Mountains (chairman of the UK Polar Committee, 1934). All of the members of the expedition were later represented in Rymill Coast and glaciers or other features along George VI Sound: Bertram; Chapman; and Fleming Glaciers.

By the beginning of the Second World War the whole coastline from the northwest of Alexander Island, northwards to the tip of the Antarctic Peninsula, and down the east coast as far as Seal Nunataks, had been explored and at least roughly charted. The South Shetland and South Orkney islands were similarly known. However, almost all this exploration had been done from the sea and beyond the glaciers and prominent peaks visible from the coast, the interior remained unknown.

Age of the whalers

By the early 1890s whaling in the Atlantic Arctic, an industry dominated by Norway and Scotland, was in decline due to over-exploitation and attention turned to the possibilities of the Southern Ocean as a new whaling ground. In the early 1890s whaling companies funded two important expeditions, one from Dundee and one from Norway, to search for whales in the northern Weddell Sea area.

The Dundee Whaling Expedition, 1892–93, led by Alexander Fairweather, had two ships that split up to cover more ocean. The *Active* circumnavigated Dundee Island (Scottish city and whaling centre) passing through Active Sound and Firth of Tay (Dundee river), whilst the *Balaena* pushed south past Seymour Island.

The Norwegian Whaling Expedition, 1892–94, was led by Carl Larsen. Over the summers of 1892–93 and 1893–94 Larsen explored the unknown east coast of Graham Land, sighting the ice shelf that now bears his name and reaching beyond the Antarctic Circle. This is an amazing achievement in the notoriously ice-bound Weddell Sea. Larsen published detailed maps after the expedition, in which he applied 12 new names to the major features of the east coast, including: Oscar II Coast (King of Sweden and Norway); Robertson Island, Lindenberg Island and Christensen Nunatak (whaling company owners); Jason Peninsula (Larsen's ship); Foyn Point (inventor of the explosive whale harpoon).

These expeditions were highly successful and led directly to the Southern Ocean whaling industry, led by Norwegian and British companies. It began in South Georgia, but expanded south to the South Shetland Islands, South Orkney Islands and Antarctic Peninsula waters from about 1905.

WHALING EXPEDITIONS 1905–31

In the beginning, whaling involved catcher ships towing the whale carcasses back to onshore stations for processing on land. The main places for this were Deception Island in the South Shetland Islands and Signy Island in the South Orkneys. Later, factory ships were developed that could process the whales on board. At first these ships had to be moored close to land for the whales to be cut up in calm waters and to get water for processing. Admiralty Bay (South Shetland Islands) and Mikkelsen Harbour, Port Lockroy, Foyn Harbour and Paradise Harbour (Graham Land) were all used as sheltered harbours for this. Eventually, starting in 1926, fully independent factory ships were developed. These featured a slipway for hauling the carcasses on board and the ability to make the large quantities of water needed for processing the whales at sea. These developments led to the decline of the shore-based stations and eventually pelagic (open sea) whaling spread throughout the Southern Ocean leading to the near-extinction of the larger whale species. Scientists estimate that right, blue and humpback whales were reduced to about 1% of their original numbers by the 1960s.

Several of the whaling captains kept detailed log books, notes and annotated charts, so that about 40 names in the South Shetland Islands and Antarctic Peninsula originate from the whalers, but they almost certainly used many more, and more names associated with whaling have been added later (Waterboat Point – named after a whalers' waterboat abandoned there). Similarly there are about 35 whaling names in the South Orkney Islands, mainly around Signy Island.

The whalers' names mainly commemorate factory ships or their catchers (Neko Harbour, Solstreif Island, Dove Channel, Orne Harbour, Orwell Glacier); captains and whale-catcher harpoonists, who were the 'star strikers' or quarterbacks of the industry (Borge Bay, Skontorp Cove, Mikkelsen Harbour, Moe Island, Jebsen Point); or the whaling itself (Whalers Bay, Factory Cove, Flensing Islands). Some names for offshore rocks and narrow channels give an inkling of the hazards of chasing whales in storm-lashed seas and through poorly charted waters: Neptunes Bellows (winds blasting through the narrow entrance to Deception Island); Sewing-Machine Needles (hazardous rocks); Hell Gates (a channel off Livingston Island, just wide enough for a whale boat).

THE DISCOVERY INVESTIGATIONS, 1925–39

In an attempt to put whaling onto a sustainable footing, the British Colonial Office began a programme of research into the natural history of whales and, by extension, the Southern Ocean ecosystem. The research used three ships between 1925 and 1939, the *Discovery, Discovery II* and *William Scoresby* and was named the Discovery Investigations accordingly. The ships criss-crossed the ocean around the Antarctic Peninsula and every opportunity was taken to improve navigational charts and gather information about anchorages to benefit the whaling industry. Whilst the Discovery Investigations did not create a great number of new place names themselves, they confirmed many names in use by the whalers and previous expeditions on new charts. Most of the scientists and ships crews have since received names as part of later mapping and charting: Cape Mackintosh and Ommaney Bay (senior scientists); Ardley Island (a hydrographic surveyor).

Place names and the age of scientific exploration

The Antarctic Peninsula gained strategic importance during World War II and the UK permanent presence in the British Antarctic Territory began with the war-time Operation Tabarin from January 1944. During this time, several bases were established in the northern Antarctic

Peninsula, including Port Lockroy (see p. 112) to deny sheltered harbours to enemy forces and to protect South Atlantic seaways. After the war the Falkland Islands Dependencies Survey (FIDS) was formed and rapidly expanded activity in the Antarctic Peninsula, including establishing several new bases spread between Admiralty Bay in the South Shetland Islands and Fossil Bluff on Alexander Island in the south. These became hubs for overland travel, so that through programmes of surveying, mapping and scientific research, the FIDS began to explore systematically the largely unknown interior and east coast.

Exploratory aerial photography flights by the US Navy began in 1947 and continued through the 1960s until superseded for regional reconnaissance by the advent of satellite imagery. A major FIDS campaign of systematic, mapping-quality aerial photography in 1956–58 achieved complete coverage of the South Shetland Islands and the west coast of the Peninsula north of Camp Point at about 68° S. Together, these airborne programmes allowed the first overview of the whole region, and the ability to relate features previously mapped on separate surveys to each other, which provided a step-change in geographical knowledge. At the same time, programmes of hydrographic charting gathered accurate information about the exact shape of the coastline and islands, and the positions of offshore rocks and reefs. This programme of exploration led to a surge in place naming, as whole mountain ranges, prominent peaks, large glaciers and other topographic features were seen for the first time.

The UK Antarctic Place-names Committee (APC) was formed in 1945 in anticipation of this surge in naming to impose some order and forward planning on place names on the Antarctic Peninsula. There are now about 4,000 UK place names in the region, ranging from Aagaard Glacier to Cape Zumberge, of which about 3,000 are in Graham Land and the South Shetland Islands. Many of the names show considerable wit and the dry humour characteristic of polar travellers: Eagle Island group; Fullastern Rock; Dismal Island; Stayaway Skerries and Achilles Heel – a subsidiary peak to Mount Achilles.

The names can be very evocative of the hardship endured in the days of long dog-sledge journeys into the unknown, and are probably the result of lamp-lit discussions over mugs of tea in storm-bound tents: Cape Disappointment; Exasperation Inlet; Blow-me-down Bluff;

BELOW

Eagle Island, east of Trinity Peninsula, showing the remarkable resemblance to an eagle in flight and the association with beak, tongue, tail, egg and eyrie features.

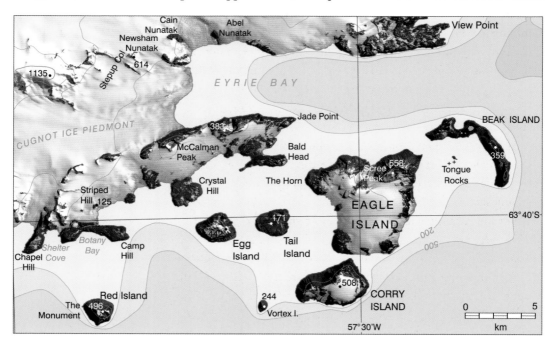

and many more. Alternatively, Dream Island and Picnic Passage recall days when things went well. Some place names visualise concisely the spectacular terrain, such as The Amphitheatre, Citadel Bastion, The Dragons Teeth, The Black Thumb, The Needles, Reptile Ridge, Witches Cauldron and Damocles Point (overhanging ice cliffs).

It soon became clear that descriptive names and naming features after expedition members would quickly become exhausted, making duplicate names difficult to avoid. In response, the UK Antarctic Place-names Committee developed the idea of clustering names into themes (see map p. 134). There are now over 40 such groups of names and examples include: Composers; pioneers of aviation, medicine, photography and ski-mountaineering; characters from Dickens, Jules Verne, Melville (Moby Dick); astronomy; Greek myth; and glaciologists.

There are very few commercial names on the Antarctic Peninsula. This is surprising given the importance of well-designed and well-proven equipment to the Antarctic traveller, and the reliance on specialist instruments by surveyors and scientists. Mobiloil Inlet, Mount Tucker, Bombardier Glacier (manufacturers of over-snow vehicles), Weasel Hill, Skidoo Nunatak, Muskeg Gap (types of vehicle) are examples of the few that exist.

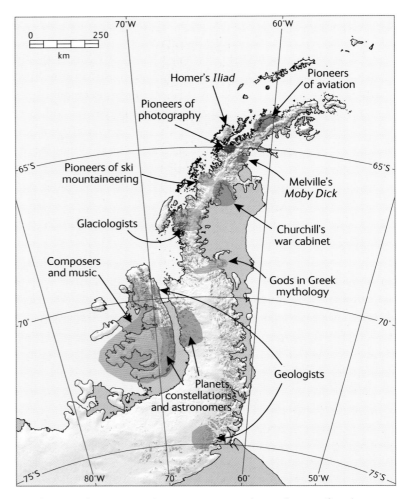

The British Antarctic Survey continues the tradition of exploratory surveys and scientific research but is no longer alone in the area. During the post-war era many other nations began to establish permanent bases in the Antarctic Peninsula region and undertake topographic mapping and related place-naming campaigns. The South Shetland Islands are one of the most accessible places to maintain an Antarctic research station and there are now about 20 stations from 11 countries in this island group. In some places this has led to the same feature having three or four names by different countries and confusion that is difficult to resolve.

Place names in the modern era

There is a continuing need for names and there are still many un-named features including mountains and glaciers. More detailed working in previously visited areas needs more precision in the naming. Improved logistics, evolving science requirements and more international collaboration mean scientists are now working in areas hitherto unexplored. The UK Antarctic Place-names Committee has already existed for more than 70 years and still has an important role in managing the place names to meet these changing requirements. Several recent names highlight prominent people: The Princess Royal Range and Attenborough Strait (Sir David Attenborough – naturalist and science broadcaster). The IAATO islands recognise the contribution to Antarctic affairs of the International Association of Antarctica Tour Operators by advocating and promoting safe and environmentally-responsible private-sector travel to the Antarctic. Place names are irrelevant unless easily accessible for practical use, so as well as appearing on published maps, the UK place names are available through an online gazetteer and web-map, showing the names on a zoomable topographic map backdrop (https://apc. antarctica.ac.uk/).

Since its first sighting by William Smith in February 1819, the Antarctic Peninsula region has gone from being completely unknown with no place names, to continent-wide coverage by modern regional-scale maps and satellite imagery, with most major topographic features having names. Antarctica may be at the end of the Earth, but the other chapters in this guide show that it has an important role in the Earth system. As international scientists seek to understand this role, they are continuing the traditions of the pioneering expeditions of the past two centuries, by both venturing into new areas to answer new science questions, and working in more detail elsewhere. This scientific fieldwork, and its supporting logistics, will always need to refer clearly and precisely to places, and there will be a continuing need to name the un-named.

ORIGINS OF PLACE NAMES FOR MOST VISITED PLACES

Aitcho Islands	Named in 1935 by the Discovery Investigations after the Admiralty Hydrographic Office – 'the H-O'.
Ardley Island	Charted in 1935 during the Discovery Investigations and named after Lieut. Richard Ardley, of Discovery II.
Cuverville Island	Charted by the Belgian Antarctic Expedition in February 1898 and named after Vice-admiral Cavelier de Cuverville of the French Navy.
Danco Island	Sighted by the Belgian Antarctic Expedition in February 1898 and named, in association with Danco Coast after Lieut. Emile Danco of the Belgian expedition.
Deception island	Named by Palmer, November 1820, with reference to the deceptive appearance of the island which conceals a superb natural harbour.
Detaille Island	Charted by the French Antarctic Expedition, it was named after M. Detaille, a French resident of Punta Arenas and shareholder in the Magellan Whaling Company, who assisted the expedition to obtain supplies at Deception Island.
Devil Island	Mapped by the Swedish Antarctic Expedition in October 1903, and named Djävulsön (Devil's Island) from its inhospitable appearance.
Hannah Point	Named in 1959, following aerial photography and surveying by the Falkland Islands Dependencies Survey, after the sealing ship *Hannah* which was wrecked in the South Shetland Islands in 1820.
Paulet Island	Charted by Ross on 30 December 1842 and named after fellow Naval officer Capt. Lord George Paulet. Occupied by the SwAE following the loss of their ship *Antarctic* in the pack ice of Erebus and Terror Gulf in February 1903.
Petermann Island	Roughly charted by the German Antarctic Expedition 1873–74 and named after Augustus Petermann, German geographer and cartographer.
Pléneau Island	Named by the French Antarctic Expedition 1903–05, after Paul Pléneau, expedition photographer.
Port Lockroy	Charted by the French Antarctic Expedition in February 1904 and named after Etienne Lockroy, a French politician who helped to finance the expedition. The bay held a FIDS station (1944–62), which is now a Historic Site and a museum operated by the UK Antarctic Heritage Trust.
Stonington Island	Site of the US Antarctic Service expedition's East Base (1939–41) and named by the expedition after Stonington Connecticut, the home port of Palmer's ship Hero. A British base was also established on the island (1946–1975).

NOTE
Brown Bluff, Half Moon Island, Horseshoe Island, Penguin Island, Shingle Cove, Snow Hill Island and Turret Point are places that are commonly visited. They are not listed in this tables as they are named descriptively.

ORIGINS OF PLACE NAMES FOR MAJOR FEATURES

Adelaide Island	Discovered in February 1832 by Biscoe who named it after Adelaide, Queen Consort of King William IV of England.
Anvers Island	Discovered by Biscoe on 21 February 1832 but named Île Anvers by de Gerlache for Antwerp, Belgium, which contributed towards the cost of the Belgian Antarctic Expedition (1897–99).
Bransfield Strait	Discovered by Edward Bransfield in January 1820, but thought to be a gulf (large bay). Named by James Weddell 1825.
Erebus and Terror Gulf	Roughly charted by James Clark Ross, December 1842–January 1843 and named after the expedition's ships.
Gerlache Strait	Charted by the Belgian Antarctic Expedition, 23 January–12 February 1898. Named after Lieut. Adrien de Gerlache de Gomery, Commander of the expedition, by the BeAE Scientific Commission at the request of the expedition members.
Graham Land	First sighted in 1820 by Bransfield and then Palmer, and named Palmer Land. It was not named Graham Land until February 1832 by Biscoe, in association with Graham Coast, after Sir James Graham, former First Lord of the Admiralty and British Home Secretary.
James Ross Island	Discovered as an island and surveyed by the Swedish Antarctic Expedition, October 1903. Named after Rear-Adm. Sir James Clark Ross, Royal Navy and British polar explorer.
Larsen Ice Shelf	Discovered in 1893 by the Norwegian whaler Carl Larsen. Roughly mapped by the Swedish Antarctic Expedition on a sledge journey in October 1902 and named after Larsen, then captain of the expedition ship *Antarctic*.
Marguerite Bay	Named by Charcot, French Antarctic Expedition 1908–10, after his wife.
Palmer Land	After being referred to as being part of Graham Land for many years, it was officially named in 1964 after Capt Nathaniel B. Palmer.
South Orkney Islands	Independently sighted by Powell on 6 December 1821 and McLeod on 12 December 1821. Named by Weddell in February 1822, in association with the South Shetland Islands and reflecting the relative positions of the northern hemisphere Shetland Islands and Orkney Islands.
South Shetland Islands	First sighted by William Smith on 19 February 1819. He named the islands in relation to the Shetland Islands in the northern hemisphere, which lie at about the same latitude.
Torgersen Island	Named by Falkland Islands Dependencies Survey in 1958 after Torstein Torgersen, First mate of the ship *Norsel* which was chartered to establish the nearby FIDS base at Arthur Harbour.
Winter Island	Named by British Graham Land Expedition, the expedition over-wintered here in 1935 with the ship *Penola*.
Yankee Harbour	The name stems from its use as a base of operations by American sealers in the 1820–21 season.

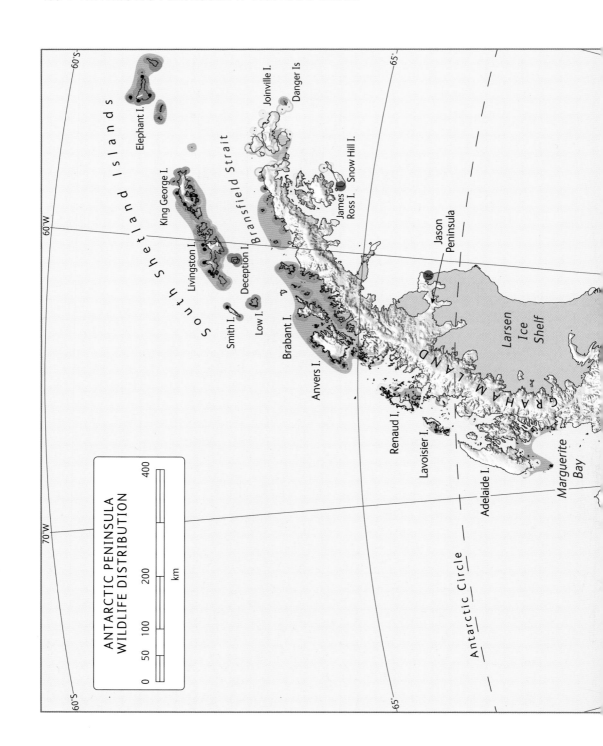

ANTARCTIC PENINSULA
WILDLIFE DISTRIBUTION

km

0   50   100   200   400

Elephant I.

South Shetland Islands

King George I.

Livingston I.

Smith I.

Deception I.

Low I.

Bransfield Strait

Joinville I.

Danger Is

James
Ross I.   Snow Hill I.

Jason
Peninsula

Brabant I.

Anvers I.

GRAHAMLAND

Larsen
Ice
Shelf

Renaud I.

Lavoisier I.

Adelaide I.

Marguerite
Bay

Antarctic Circle

60°S

60°W

70°W

60°S

65°

65°

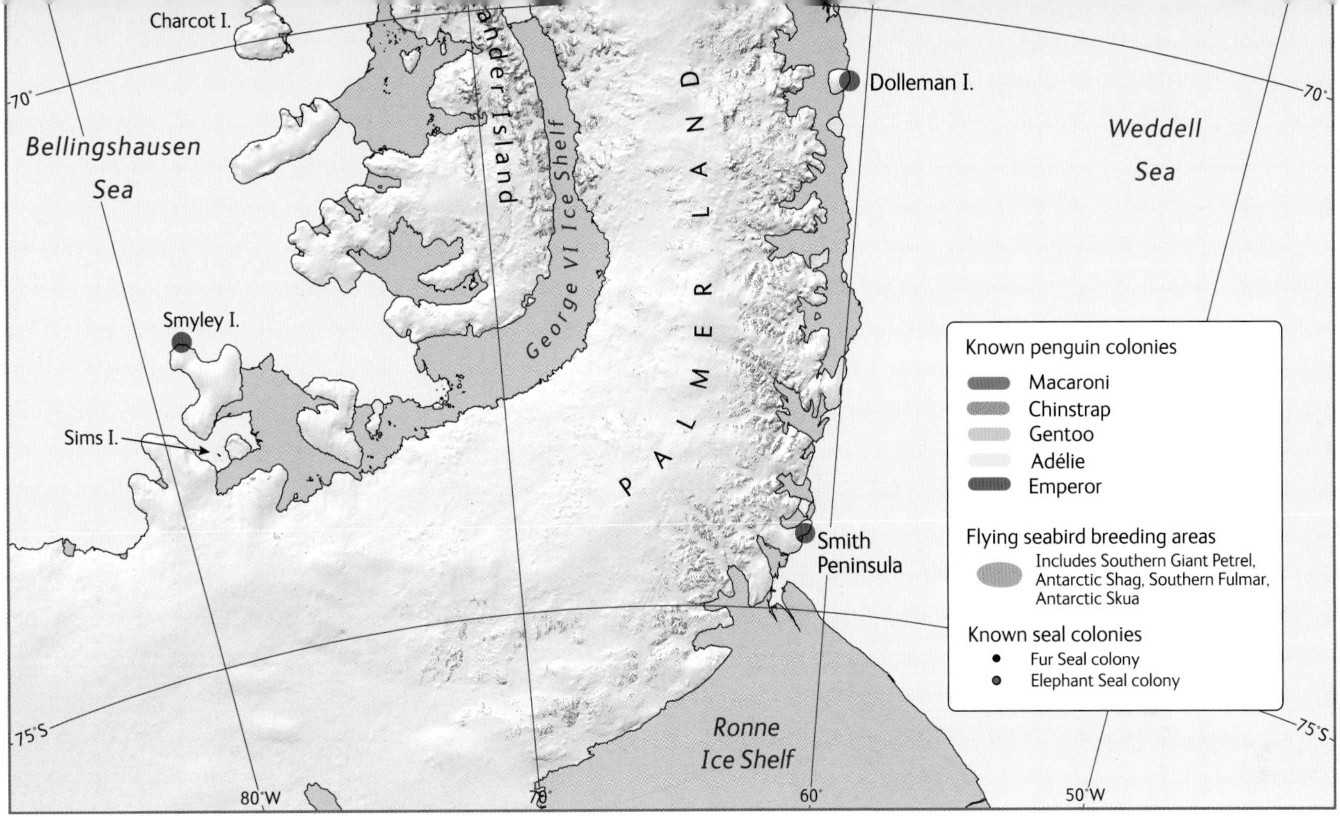

Known penguin colonies
- Macaroni
- Chinstrap
- Gentoo
- Adélie
- Emperor

Flying seabird breeding areas
Includes Southern Giant Petrel, Antarctic Shag, Southern Fulmar, Antarctic Skua

Known seal colonies
- Fur Seal colony
- Elephant Seal colony

Weddell Sea

Dolleman I.

Smith Peninsula

Ronne Ice Shelf

P A L M E R   L A N D

George VI Ice Shelf

...ander Island

Charcot I.

Bellingshausen Sea

Smyley I.

Sims I.

70°

75°S

50°W

60°

80°W

75°S

70°

ABOVE
This map of known major breeding colonies of penguins, flying birds and seals highlights areas where they are most likely to be seen in large numbers during the Antarctic summer. It shows the zonation in distribution of penguin species, with ice-intolerant species such as gentoo and chinstrap in the north and west, with the so-called, ice-obligate species emperor and adélie in the colder south and east.

INDEX

FURTHER INFORMATION

www.bas.ac.uk The British Antarctic Survey website. A wealth of information about Antarctica, as well as details about BAS science and operations and access to the BAS picture library.

www.discoveringantarctica.org.uk Information about Antarctica aimed at school students and the general reader.

www.gov.uk/world/organisations/ british-antarctic-territory Information about Antarctica from the UK Foreign and Commonwealth Office Polar Regions Department, with links to other organisations active in the Antarctic Peninsula region.

www.scar.org The Scientific Committee on Antarctic Research. Detailed information about international scientific research in Antarctica and comprehensive links to educational and general interest resources.

www.spri.cam.ac.uk The Scott Polar Research Institute. Resources about the history of Antarctica, expeditions and an extensive picture library.

www.ukaht.org Information about the history of the Antarctic Peninsula region and the conservation work of the UK Antarctic Heritage Trust.

MAPS

British Antarctic Survey map catalogue: Details about topographic and geological maps, including details on how to buy: **www.bas.ac.uk/data/our-data/maps/**

Graham Land and South Shetland Islands/ Scotia Sea. British Antarctic Survey. 2017. ISBN: 978-0-856652103. This double-sided map provides an overview of the northern Antarctic Peninsula area on side A, with a regional-scale map covering the Scotia Sea on side B. It is an ideal companion for a voyage from South America or the Falkland Islands to the Antarctic Peninsula.

Scientific Committee on Antarctic Research Map Catalogue: An online listing of international maps of Antarctica: **https://data.aad.gov.au/ aadc/mapcat/**

Scientific Committee on Antarctic Research Antarctic Digital Database: An online digital map of Antarctica compiled from the best available international mapping, with place name and location search: **www.add.scar.org/**

BOOKS AND WEBSITES

GEOLOGY OF GRAHAM LAND

Geology and Geomorphology of Deception Island. Smellie, J.L., López-Martínez, J. and others. British Antarctic Survey, 2002. ISBN: 9780856651762. A 78-page book and detailed maps.

WEATHER AND CLIMATE

Antarctic Meteorology and Climatology. King, J.C. and Turner, J. Cambridge University Press, 2007. ISBN: 9780521039840.

Atmospheric Optical phenomena: **www.atoptics.co.uk/**

NASA Ozone Hole Watch **http://ozonewatch.gsfc.nasa.gov/**

THE ICE SHEET

Glaciers. Hambrey, M. and Alean, J. Cambridge University Press, 2nd edn, 2011. ISBN: 9780521828086. An accessible and well-illustrated introduction to glaciers and glacial phenomena.

ICEBERGS AND SEA ICE

A Field Guide to Ice. Fenton, J.H.C. Footprints of Abernyte & Inverasdale, 2009. ISBN: 9780953006946. This booklet is a useful photo-guide to polar landscapes, and includes sections on sea ice and icebergs.

Ice in the Ocean. Wadhams, P. Gordon and Breach Science Publishers, 2000. ISBN: 9789056992965. A comprehensive textbook examining sea ice, icebergs and their role in the global climate system.

Polar View: Online access to up-to-date information about sea ice conditions on the Antarctic Peninsula: **www.polarview.aq**

LIFE ON LAND

The Biology of Polar Regions. Thomas, D.N., Fogg, G., Convey, P., Fritsen, C., Gilli, J.M., Gradinger, R., Laybourne-Parry, J., Reid, K. and Walton, D.W.H. Oxford University Press, 2008. ISBN: 9780199298112. An accessible introduction to polar ecosystems – marine and terrestrial, north and south.

Life at Extremes. Bell, E. (ed.). CABI Publishing, 2012. ISBN: 9781845938147. An introduction and overview to extreme environments.

Low Temperature Biology of Insects. Denlinger, D.L. and Lee, R.E., Jr. (eds.). Cambridge University Press, 2010. ISBN: 9780521886352. Insects' adaptations to extreme environments.

Trends in Antarctic Terrestrial and Limnetic Ecosystems: Antarctica as a Global Indicator. Bergstrom, D.M., Convey, P. and Huiskes, A.H.L. (eds.). Springer, 2006. ISBN: 9781402052767. An overview of biological responses to climate change in Antarctica.

A LAND OF CHANGE

Antarctic Climate Change and the Environment. Turner, J., Bindschadler, R.A., Convey, P., Di Prisco, G., Fahrbach, E., Gutt, J., Hodgson, D.A., Mayewski, P.A. and Summerhayes, C.P. (eds). Scientific Committee on Antarctic Research, 2009. ISBN: 9780948277221. Available online at: **www.scar.org/**

THE ANTARCTIC TREATY

The Antarctic Treaty Secretariat website. Information about the Antarctic Treaty and the Environmental Protocol: **www.ats.aq**

Politics in a Cold Climate: Antarctic Science and Governance. Walton, D.W.H. and Dudeney, J. Cambridge University Press, 2017. ISBN: 9780521170413.

PLACE NAMES

The History of Place-names in the British Antarctic Territory. Hattersley-Smith, G. British Antarctic Survey, 1991. ISBN: 9780856651303.

Southern Horizons: The History of the British Antarctic Territory. Burton, R. UK Antarctic Heritage Trust, 2008. ISBN: 9780954138912.

The UK Antarctic Place-names Committee website and web-map. Information about the location and origins of UK place names on the Antarctic Peninsula: **https://apc.antarctica.ac.uk/**

AUTHOR BIOGRAPHIES

PROFESSOR PETER CONVEY is an 'Individual Merit' research scientist at the British Antarctic Survey, specialising in terrestrial ecology and biogeography of the polar regions. He has participated in 15 Antarctic research seasons. He is a member of the UK National Committee on Antarctic Research, and is very active in the development of international Antarctic science priorities and collaborative research programmes through the Scientific Committee on Antarctic Research.

STUART DOUBLEDAY is Deputy Head of the Foreign and Commonwealth Office's Polar Regions Department and Administrator of the British Antarctic Territory. He represents the UK at the annual Antarctic Treaty Consultative Meetings and is the UK Representative to the Committee for Environmental Protection.

DR ADRIAN FOX is Head of Mapping and Geographic Information at the British Antarctic Survey and has led more than 10 fieldwork campaigns in the Antarctic Peninsula region. He is Co-Chair of the international Scientific Committee on Antarctic Geographic Information. He is Secretary to the UK Antarctic Place-names Committee and is interested in the history of mapping and place names in Antarctica.

PROFESSOR DAME JANE FRANCIS is Director of BAS and an expert on Antarctic fossil forests and the evidence that they provide on past climate evolution.

DR PHILIP T LEAT is a geologist and Honorary Research Fellow at the British Antarctic Survey. He has visited Antarctica and the Scotia Sea 12 times to carry out geological fieldwork. He is interested in submarine volcanoes, the geochemistry of volcanic rocks and the geological evolution of Antarctica.

JONATHAN SHANKLIN is an Honorary Research Fellow at the British Antarctic Survey and was previously Head of the Meteorology and Ozone Monitoring Unit. During his time with the survey he made 19 visits to Antarctica, 12 of them including visits to the Antarctic Peninsula. He was a member of the BAS team that discovered the Antarctic Ozone Hole.

DR JOHN SHEARS joined the British Antarctic Survey in 1990 as Antarctic Environmental Officer and became Head of Operations and Engineering at BAS, and the lead for the UK on operational issues at Antarctic Treaty meetings, between 2010 and 2014.

PROFESSOR DAVID VAUGHAN, OBE joined the British Antarctic Survey in 1985 as a glaciologist and is now Director of Science. He has worked widely on the retreat of Antarctic Peninsula ice shelves. He has been an author in the last two assessment reports by the Intergovernmental Panel on Climate Change.

DRAKE PASSAGE

SOUTH SHETLAND ISLANDS

55°W

60°W

65°W

65°S

Sealers Passage 53.

Clarence Island

Elephant Island

Loper Channel

74

Gibbs I.

Aspland I.

King George Island

Snow I.

C. Shirreff

Livingston I.

Greenwich I.

Robert I.

Nelson I.

Nelson Str.

3 4

5 6

2

9 8

7

1

Deception I.

Smith Island

Mt. Foster 2100

Boyd Strait

Low I.

BRANSFIELD STRAIT

Hoseason I.

Astrolabe I.

Tower I.

Trinity I.

d'Urville I.

Bransfield I.

Joinville I.

Dundee I.

Danger Is.

Paulet I.

41

O'Higgins 37 (Chile)

Antarctic Sd.

Esperanza 39 (Arg.)

Eagle I.

Vega I.

Marambio (Arg.)

60

Seymour I.

38

Snow Hill I.

James Ross Island

Erebus and Terror Gulf

WEDDELL

Trinity Pen.

Prince Gustav Channel

C. Longing

Larsen Inlet

Sobral Pen.

Site of Larsen A Ice Shelf

Seal Nunataks

Robertson I.

Site of Larsen B Ice Shelf

Exasperation Inlet

Vaughan Inlet

45

Detroit Plateau

Orleans Strait

Gerlache Strait

Brabant Island

29

G56

Flandres Bay

28

Lemaire Ch.

27

Anvers Island

Palmer (USA)

Mt Français 2825

61,84

Vernadsky (Ukr.) 62

Graham Plateau

2000

1000

2000

3000

5000

2000

1000

65°S

A   N   T   A   R   C   T   I   C

Historic sites and monuments, South Shetland Islands

51

50,52,

82,86

36

33,34,35

57

31,58,

71

91

59

76
